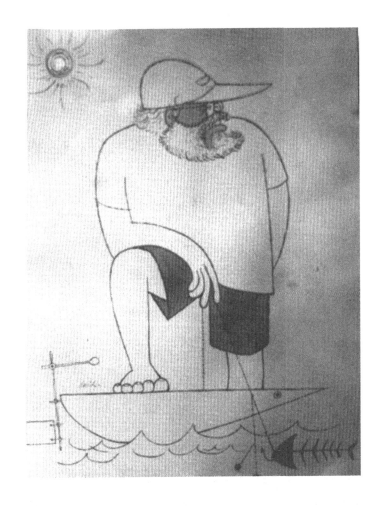

That Other Hemingway

The master inventor

JAMES D. BRASCH

 www.trafford.com

North America & international
toll-free: 1 888 232 4444 (USA & Canada)
phone: 250 383 6864 • fax: 812 355 4082

Notes on the Cover

When Mary Hemingway returned to Cuba after Hemingway's death in order to remove manuscripts and personal belongings before the *Finca Vigia* was turned over to the Cuban government, she also obtained permission to remove the collection of modernist paintings that hung on the walls of the old house. At first, Mrs. Hemingway was told by Cuban officials that works of art could not be removed from socialist countries. She therefore applied directly to Fidel Castro and insisted that the paintings were her personal property since Hemingway had given them to her at various times as presents. As she explained it to us:

> So I got onto Fidel and explained to him that Ernest had—and this was really true—see Ernest never remembered my birthday-very seldom. So I would say, "Let's have a glass of champagne before lunch today, Sweet," and his face would fall: "I've forgotten something."

> "Is this our wedding anniversary?" "No, Dear."

> And then suddenly he'd remember and would lift a picture off the wall and with a, you know, with a kleenix or something dust it off and solemnly come to wherever I was, saying "Happy birthday."

And I would say "Thank you, darling," and we'd then re-hang it wherever it had been hanging.

And so I was being truthful to Fidel, saying these were personal presents of Ernest to me and were my private property and I felt I was entitled to take them. And he assigned an army officer to see I got my stuff, including my desk, which was, by far, the biggest object, shipped up to, I think it was Tampa. Anyway on the last, it happened to be the very last, commercial boat leaving Havana harbor before the embargo. (Mary Hemingway to JDB and JS, taped conversation, Jan 22, 1977)

When the Cuban authorities were preparing to open the *Finca Vigia* to the public as a Hemingway Museum, they faced the problem of the bare walls. The only pictures Mary Hemingway had left behind were a small bullfight picture by Robert Domingo, a few prints of famous paintings, and several large framed bullfight posters. The house looked very different from Hemingway's time when stunning works by Klee, Miró, and Braque among others hung on the walls.

One of the most interesting replacements was a humorous portrayal of Hemingway as the Old Man of the Sea by the Cuban artist, Juan David Many attempts have been made at one time or another to parody Hemingway's content and style. The most extensive series of humorous drawings and paintings of Hemingway were by his close friend, Waldo Peirce. After Peirce, however, David seems to me to be the most successful artist to try his hand at a satirical portrait of Hemingway.

Juan David, a Cuban communist, was the master cartoonist of Cuba. His teacher, Masaguer, a famous Cuban caricaturist and Masaguer's other student, Antonio Rubio, are now both dead. The wit of the David cartoon may be something of a surprise to those who associate communist art with social realism and the ponderous portrayal of heroic workers. However, while in Cuba we visited the Museo Nacional in Havana and were impressed by the strong element of fantasy and humor in the painting and ceramics by young Cuban artists in the contemporary Cuban gallery.

At *Finca Vigia* David's caricature was hung on the wall of the dining room directly across from Hemingway's normal place at the table. This is the same spot where Miró's *The Farm* hung earlier. Although caricature is a far cry from the Miró painting, it is only fair to note that Hemingway himself did seem to have considerable interest in the art of the cartoon. His library contained sixteen collections of cartoons by such eminent practitioners as Peter Arno, Charles Addams and the Cuban, Gustavo Grau Mederos.

"…..He could invent from knowledge."

Hemingway on Tolstoy

Again,

For Delores

Table of Contents

Preface

Recent news out of Cuba and the Rockefeller Fund indicate that over 3,000 items owned by Ernest Hemingway are about to be released to the public. Since my work has already revealed the extent of Hemingway's library I am excited about this material which was withheld from me by the Division of Museums and Monuments when I worked at *Finca Vigia* to produce *Hemingway's Library* (1981) I am aware that my publications (some along with Joeseph Sigman) on Hemingway, would form a useful guide and context and provide insight into what these letters and other items are likely to reveal.

The work on the library, including the 7368 books known to have been owned by Hemingway at the time of his death, has been posted on the internet by the John F. Kennedy Library, but hard copies of the original volume are almost impossible to obtain. I am sure that the portrait of Hemingway presented in these materials would seriously challenge a great deal of current and earlier scholarship and biographical details of Hemingway's life. The correspondence with Bernard Berenson, Malcolm Cowley and the dependence on Dr. Herrera are particularly significant in that they represent the intellectual atmosphere in which Hemingway read and wrote. What is important at this moment is that this material which informs his isolated and lonely habitat in Cuba is virtually unavailable. The Herrera material is available at the present time only in Russian. The Cowley material has disappeared from the scholarly and public domain. The Hemingway/Berenson correspondence is only available in the secluded villa north of Florence, Italy.

For a review of his reading life and the description of his library see the Introduction to *Hemingway's Library: A Composite Record (1981).* The extent which Hemingway depended on this great accumulation of knowledge, depended on his wife Mary and these close friends. Many other individuals could be added, but these three are particularly rewarding as we consider his intellectual life and loneliness in Cuba.

Introduction

In October 1976, scholars from the United States, Europe and Canada met at the University of Alabama for a symposium to "revaluate" Hemingway. Several decades of psychological mining and biographical debris had provided the chief source for critical commentary, and scholars were beginning to discover that many aspects of Hemingway's novels and short stories had been ignored because of the exaggerated emphasis on biography. Most revealing had been the recent work of Jackson J. Benson, Sheldon Grebstein, Linda Wagner and Emily Stipes Watts (see my review essay, "Hemingway's Words: Enduring James' Thoughts," *Modernist Studies*, Vol. 2, No.1, pp. 45-50). The conference was graced by the presence of Mary Welsh Hemingway who spoke charmingly of the many literary men in her life (she intentionally did not mention Hemingway) and then gently chided those assembled for their interest in "hidden meanings" which she insisted that she seldom noticed. Casually, during a question period, she dropped a few hints of her own. Hemingway's favorite poet, for example, was Charles Baudelaire and the still intact library at *Finca Vigia, San Francisco de Paula*, Cuba, contained two annotated copies of *Les Fleurs du Mal*. After a few more comments, efforts to get into the library accelerated. A number of scholars had already tried to penetrate off-limits Cuba, but Americans were not permitted to travel there and the Cubans were inhospitable to prying researchers. A mysterious microfiche of a carbon copy of the "official" inventory of the books in *Finca Vigia* obtained by a German scholar contained many errors, was frequently illegible on many of its almost 1,100 pages and, most significantly, was not available to anybody.

Adding to the information on Hemingway's books and manuscripts was Jo August, curator of the Hemingway collection at the Kennedy Library then in Waltham, Massachusetts. The speaker's roster also included Matthew Bruccoli, Alfred Kazin and Philip Young. Ample opportunity was provided for the announced reassessment of the state of critical affairs, but two papers more than any others clearly illustrated that the conference would be remembered as the watershed in the history of Hemingway scholarship.

Representing the "old school" of biographical/psychological criticism was Scott Donaldson (The College of William and Mary), whose paper, "Frederick Henry, Selfish Lover," summarized existing character analysis, biographical parallels and the intermingling of Lieut. Henry and Ernest Hemingway which had preoccupied the disciples and descendants of Philip Young and Carlos Baker. Michael S. Reynolds' (North Carolina State University) analysis of the manuscript of *The Sun Also Rises*, in his paper, "False Dawn: The First Draft Beginning of *The Sun Also Rises*," focused attention on the new directions: research on the manuscripts now available in the Kennedy Library and a recognition of the linguistic and aesthetic dimensions of Hemingway's works resulting from a consideration of his work in the light of his interests in Cezanne, Goya, Eliot, Pound, Joyce and Gertrude Stein, among others. Fortunately, book length treatments of both orientations are now available. Scott Donaldson's paper is the basis of chapter vii of *By Force of Will: The Life and Art of Ernest Hemingway*, (1977). Michael S. Reynolds' paper is now published, but his meticulous research on the manuscripts and his profound understanding of the relation between art and life as used by Hemingway for the purposes of "conventions" is amply illustrated by *Hemingway's First War: The Making of "A Farewell to Arms* (1976). Scott Donaldson's study of Hemingway's life and art focuses on what others have already written about the "life" and gives only casual and unconvincing space to "art." As a matter of record, art seems to be ignored in favor of yet another reconsideration of the parallels which exist between Hemingway's heroes and his own biography. Frequently the novels and short stories are used to illustrate some insight into Hemingway, instead of Hemingway's biography being used to clarify some point in a story. For many years the biographical method has been held up to some suspicion, but since the Alabama symposium, the method has become highly suspect when applied to Hemingway. In his defense it might be added that Donaldson's book was probably at the printers by the time the symposium took place.

Donaldson's urbane tone, his questionable focus on biography and his lack of feeling for his subject may be illustrated by one of his reflections on a story which he retells about Hemingway's childhood. In a chapter on "Sport" which summarizes what others have written about Hemingway's obvious fascination with variations on athletic competition, Donaldson repeats Leicester Hemingway's sarcastic comment that as a baseball player, "Ernest was a pretty studious reader": His mother used to find him pouring over a book, and propose that he go out to play some baseball, "Aw, Mother," Ernest would answer, "I pitch like a bear," and go on reading. Donaldson uses the incident to illustrate Hemingway's bravado and bluster and goes on to chide Hemingway for his assumption of some expertise when there seems to be some reason for questioning whether he had any skill in the business of baseball at all. This might be permissible if Donaldson were writing the biography of Willy Mays, but as a reprimand to an author it is bewildering. It apparently never occurs to Donaldson that he should have tried to find out what Hemingway was reading. The incident tells us more about Donaldson and his values than it does about Hemingway. Worse, the chapter goes on to a recitation of all the sporting incidents told and retold by all those who knew "how it was" (Donaldson still includes bull-fighting as a "sport" which it certainly is not as Hemingway made abundantly clear in *Death in the Afternoon*). Moreover, Donaldson fails to recognize the art of the *corrida* as a metaphor for the art of writing. He does include in the chapter on "sport" Hemingway's admiration for Cezanne, a strange digression in a chapter devoted to sport. He has evidently just discovered a note card on Emily Stipes Watts (*Ernest Hemingway and the Arts*, 1971). Summarizing other critics seems to be Donaldson's sport.

Other chapters survey biographical details under the headings of Fame, Money, Politics, War, Love, Sex, Friendship, Religion, Art, Mastery (a particularly obtuse understanding of dramatic propriety and Hemingway's use of irony) and Death. The essays would be useful only for undergraduates who are too busy to look up the relevant topics in Baker's monumental biography, but anyone else should beware. Donaldson's loaded implications ("Hemingway tended to assume") tell more about Donaldson and his values than about Hemingway's art. His falsification of Hemingway's letters to Arthur Mizener, for example, may have a variety of excuses since they are not easily available and there is no evidence in the book that Donaldson actually read them. He may be depending on the incomplete and misleading summary which appeared in *The Saturday Review* (Oct. 2, 1976, pp. 4-6). But this is no excuse. According to Hemingway's will the letters could not be quoted, but using a passage on Hemingway's understanding of God (EH to Arthur Mizener, May 12, 1950), one of the few really fine passages of Hemingway's later years, to illustrate what Donaldson calls Hemingway's "downfall" (p. 261) is ample demonstration of the author's desire to ram Hemingway into a preconceived mold which barely suggests the master stylist and descendant of Henry James whom we have come to know as a result of recent literary, as distinct from biographical, criticism.

This is the most questionable and most irresponsible kind of biographical criticism. Examples of Donaldson's insinuations and conjectures abound, but I find particularly objectionable his use of the fiction to "document" Hemingway's life. Referring to Katy Smith (Mrs. Dos Passos), for example, Donaldson comments (p. 145): "if one takes literally a story called 'Summer People,' Ernest may have had an affair with her in the summer of 1920."

Recognizing that his evidence is inconclusive, Donaldson continues: "The least that can be said is that imaginatively Ernest possessed Katy." Whatever else might be said about such commentary, it must be stated that it seems inappropriate to ignore the imagination of the writer or what the earlier critics had called "invention" and then somehow transfer imaginative details to the "life." There is another kind of misapplication functioning when Donaldson misreads a story in order to promote his misconceptions about Hemingway. For example, he insists that Margo Macomber "guns down" her husband at the end of "The Short Happy Life of Francis Macomber" (she does not!) and that this somehow proves Hemingway's "preoccupation with death." Hemingway may have been fascinated with death, but misreading a story to demonstrate the matter does not help much.

There can be no doubt that many aspects of Hemingway's life were unpleasant and many were exciting, but all the footnotes, quotations, letters, anecdotes about sport and love will not explain how or why he wrote "Big TwoHearted River" and *A Farewell to Arms*. For that we have to look elsewhere. We also have to read what Hemingway wrote and have some sense of his technique. Plot summaries, innuendoes and a redistribution of Hemingway's life under subject headings (Hemingway's life is admittedly almost a card catalogue of America from 1900-1960) reveal that Donaldson is unaware of the new directions in Hemingway criticism: an end to biographical trivia, an end to psychological assumptions, an end to Freudian compensations as the dynamics of creation and, more important, a recognition of Hemingway's real concern for language and his debt to Henry James and Paul Cezanne, among others. At a time when the young Hemingway was conscious of a need for instruction he was fortunate to find himself in the company of James' immediate descendants: Gertrude Stein, Ezra Pound, Pablo Picasso, James Joyce and Ford Madox Ford. Hemingway scholars are now aware of this. As the totality of manuscripts in the Kennedy Library reveals, Hemingway and Henry James were kindred spirits, both consummate craftsmen concerned about the worn-out language which had carried thousands to France and northern Italy, but which would never satisfy those few who survived the slaughter.

Fortunately, the antidote was available in Michael S. Reynolds' *Hemingway's First War*,(1976) the fascinating result of painstaking research undertaken to answer some fundamental questions about Hemingway's second novel—one of the finest "lyric novels" in the language.

Reynolds began his research as a result of several questions raised about Hemingway's use of the retreat from Caporetto. Why Caporetto? How closely did Hemingway's description match the historical event? How did he select his details? Did the details correspond to available maps of the campaigns in northern Italy? The result is a complete reversal of previous commentary about Hemingway's participation in World War I, about his use of details of World War I in the novel which, in addition, provides some hard thoughts on the use of actual events of the war and their treatment in fiction. Students of World War I will find Reynolds' book a useful companion to Paul Fussell's *The Great War and Modern Memory* (1975), an examination of the literary means by which the British experience on the Western Front has been "remembered, conventionalized and mythologized." Given the current passion for fusing or confusing fact and fiction, Reynolds' book is especially important.

Reynolds' report on his research is divided into three sections: The Writer at Work (1928-1930); The Making of the Novel (1918-1928); Critical Response: Technique and Structure. The chapters are documented with detailed maps of northern Italy (keyed to passages in the novel) and remarkable photographs illustrating such details as the Italian retreat at Caporetto, Hemingway in the Red Cross hospital, and various portraits of the main source of Hemingway's inspiration for Catherine Barkley, Agnes von Kurowsky. The photos and maps of the Italian campaign are a measure of Reynolds' thoroughness and probably equal the importance of Emily Watts' analyses of Cezanne's landscape and Goya's *Disaster of War* as source studies of Hemingway's technique.

Section I proceeds from Cowley's generally ignored statement (1945) that Hemingway had not been at Caporetto and recalls Hemingway's statements about the relation of fact and fiction and how he had found it necessary to use someone else's experience of the war front. He recreated the experience of the retreat from maps, books and first-hand descriptions, especially Red Cross reports. Reynolds shows how the material was adapted to focus on Hemingway's primary concern: what remained of conventional language after the war? At about the same time as Sheldon Grebstein was studying the manuscript of *A Farewell to Arms* in the Kennedy Library (See *Hemingway's Craft*, 1973, pp. 206-07), Reynolds also was there and discovered a portion of the interview between Preston Lockwood and Henry James typed on an unnumbered page of the manuscript in the Kennedy Library. Hemingway had typed:

Henry James in conversation with Preston Lockwood

New York Times, March 21, 1915

> One finds it in the midst of all this as hard to ap-
> ply one's words as to endure one's thoughts. The war
> has used up words; they have weakened, they have
> deteriorated like motor car tires ... and we are now
> confronted with a depreciation of all our terms, or
> otherwise speaking, with a loss of expression through
> increase of limpness, that may well make us wonder
> what ghosts will be left to walk.

Reynolds recognizes that this passage illuminates one of the key
passages of *A Farewell to Arms* ("I was always embarrassed by the
words sacred, glorious and sacrifice and the expression in vain....")
and how this quotation influenced the shaping of material which
we know as *A Farewell to Arms*. Essentially Hemingway used his
sources to produce a lament for the worn-out language of the past,
dramatizing the impossibility of conventional abstract solutions in
the face of the only reality: "That was what you did. You died." (p.
338)

Of course more material than the Caporetto retreat went into the
novel, and Section II carefully reviews the material at Hemingway's
disposal. The analysis of the Italian Front in 1915-16 as reported in
contemporary accounts, the details of the retreat from Caporetto
and the search for Catherine (Agnes Von Kurowski plus Hadley plus
Pauline), reveal the sources of the Hemingway style which gained
acceptance after Hemingway learned that "hard facts create an
immediate sense of authenticity" (p. 14). Most significant, I think,
is Reynolds' exploration of Hemingway's literary sources. So far
as I can discover this was the first detailed acknowledgement and
analysis of the fact that Hemingway was a voracious reader. Reynolds
has pointed out the necessity of recording Hemingway's historical
sources both as origins for specific details in northern Italy (Douglas
W. Johnson's *Battle Fields of the World War, Baedeker's Guide to Italy*
and others) and for biographical details of his fictional characters
(*New York Times, Scribners' Magazine*, etc.). The parallels between

Lieut. Henry and Fabrizio in Stendahl's *The Charterhouse of Parma* reveal Hemingway for the consummate literary artist that he was. Hemingway picks and chooses as is necessary to force events and characters to serve his art. Unfortunately Reynolds must frequently resort to speculation on Hemingway's sources since access to Hemingway's library was forbidden. Fortunately, more evidence to support Reynolds' research was soon available. (See *Hemingway's Library*, 1981)

Section III analyzes the techniques by which Hemingway turned his documents, actual and literary experience, and other research into fiction. Reynolds passes over the characteristic prose style, presumably because it has been noted by just about everybody, and identifies three basic techniques used for the working of the material into an artistic whole: foreshadowing, the use of "echo scenes" and the habit of reversing roles between characters.

Although one might question Reynolds' suggestion that Catherine is the real heroine of the novel with Frederick Henry in the role of "anti-hero," his analysis of the novel includes an interesting application of the imagist technique of definition by negation ("I am not prince Hamlet", "I am no prophet", etc.) which Hemingway obviously learned from the generation of writers after Henry James. Lieut. Henry emerges in Reynolds' reading, not as an Italian, not Austrian, not a German infiltrator, not a hero, not an officer, not Catherine's husband, not her cousin, not a boxer, not a doctor. In short Hemingway uses the imagist technique to portray a character in absolute isolation—a condition which Reynolds not only identifies as Lieut. Henry's essential characteristic, but also the national characteristic of the United States from post World War I to the late Twenties. The parallels to today are ominous.

In his final chapter Reynolds reviews how the structure of the novel, overwhelming all other questions of sources and actual experience, reveals Frederick Henry as a non-person with no beliefs and no institutions—social or linguistic—upon which to rely. "He is the truly isolated man, and the novel's central concern has been tracing out his journey into isolation" (p. 274). We are a long way here from Hemingway's fiction being analyzed as a therapy for psychological adjustment. Reynolds' basic assumption is that to mistake art for biography is to equate illusion with reality (p. 15). Underlying all of his research is Reynolds' insistence that Hemingway "never allowed reality to interfere with his fiction, and in the early years he did not allow his personal experience to dictate to his work as an artist" (p. 170). When we recognize that Hemingway selected his material and arranged his experience to fit the needs of his fiction we have come full circle from Donaldson's use of the fiction to reveal or clarify Hemingway's biography. Basic to it all is some appreciation and admiration for the art of "invention."

One of the reasons Reynolds' study is important in the identification of the watershed in Hemingway criticism is that Reynolds was quite aware of what changes he was recording. *Hemingway's First War* is also, therefore, an essay on critical method. He is quite conscious of what his book means to future readers of Hemingway's work:

> Now that the first half of the twentieth century is no longer the "modern age," but an historical period of its own, it is time for critics to relearn the use of old tools. The vein of psychoanalytic exegesis has been overworked. The misleading thesis that Hemingway is always his own protagonist has littered the critical landscape with so much debris that it will take another generation of critics to restore the ecology. Letters, manuscripts, source reading, social milieu, and literary biography must all be brought to bear on the published text. Hemingway's reading is as important to his art as that of Coleridge; his textual revisions are as significant as those of Keats. With Hemingway it is time to question constructively all of the explications we have inherited. We must begin the difficult and frequently tedious search for the hard data that will support, modify, or disprove our inheritance. (p. 283)

Reynolds' work not only provides a perceptive reading of *A Farewell to Arms* and an understanding of how it emerged from the artist as a work of art, but he enlarges our understanding of the making of any work of art. This is no small achievement, but taken

·beside the fact that he indicates the direction which the criticism of Hemingway, and possibly of many other writers, must take in the near future, the impact of the book will even surpass its singular service to students of Ernest Hemingway's works. Most important he reveals how trivial and misleading are those critics who dissect the art of fiction for the dubious purpose of producing fictions about the artist. It is a curious quirk of twentieth century American literary criticism that the two most important novelists of the period have not had more detailed analysis in the context of each other's work. Hemingway and Faulkner and the writings celebrating their respective achievements have developed as separate countries. To be sure they contributed to this mutual isolation by the manner in which they managed biographical enquiries. Now that both have been the subjects of laborious and by and large unsatisfactory biographies, their separation is open to question. The paucity of information on Faulkner's life has always forced Faulknerians to depend on the works themselves. Now Hemingway scholars are discovering that his biography obscures more problems than it clarifies. A reexamination of both men's professional careers and a rereading of their fiction, especially Hemingway's has begun. Significantly, they are being discovered as residents and craftsmen of the same country.

Linda Wagner's *Hemingway and Faulkner: Inventors/Masters.* [Metuchen, New Jersey: The Scarecrow Press, 1975.] contribution to this reexamination is a natural extension of her two earlier volumes of Faulkner/Hemingway scholarship: *William Faulkner: Four Decades of Criticism* (1973) and *Ernest Hemingway: Five Decades of Criticism* (1974). *Five Decades* was one of the first works of Hemingway criticism to concentrate on the fiction and let the man alone, as Faulkner critics have done all along. In the later volume we have the results of this recognition and a preliminary examination of the two writers in the context of each other's work. More important, Wagner focuses on the fact that Hemingway and Faulkner were, first and foremost, brilliant craftsmen. They rose to prominence among their contemporaries because both were experimenters and both concentrated on perfecting their technique. As her title reminds us, they were the inventors and the masters. Echoes of Henry James abound.

This strangely printed and somewhat uneven book bristles with insights and observations which frequently force a reader to wonder why parallel treatment has not been the focus rather than the periphery of Hemingway/Faulkner criticism. In addition to her own assessment of their mutual importance, Wagner has distilled the critical material assembled for her earlier collections. Frequently she fills out the pattern of her own reading by directing the reader to a broad range of literary commentators who have already analyzed the technical achievements of one or both of the writers. Although there is a useful index it is unfortunate that the volume lacked a bibliography devoted to identifying those commentaries which tread the developing terrain between the two authors. It is, of course, a vast and perhaps nebulous field, but Wagner's earlier volumes place her foremost in the list of those able to compile such a bibliography.

Hemingway and Faulkner, the two most distinguished students of Sherwood Anderson, also learned from Henry James, Ezra Pound and to a lesser degree Joyce, Conrad, and Ford Madox Ford. James's focus on craft is Wagner's *donnée*. Pound's focus on the image is the key to her interpretation of their development. Substituting the scene for the image, both men sharpened their scenes to provide the disciplined view and accuracy which the imagists demanded. Wagner includes a provocative appendix on both authors as experimental poets. The impact of Ezra Pound and imagism on Hemingway, especially in *The Sun Also Rises* is crucial. Her first two chapters not only document Hemingway's debt, but reveal how an understanding of this influence leads to an understanding of how the novel works. According to Wagner, the success of *The Sun Also Rises* led to the excessive biographical interest in the author and tended to obscure his later passion for the development of his craft along the lines established in this early novel. The experimental nature of Hemingway's prose, especially the use of dialogue in *In Our Time*, leads to Wagner's later discussion of *To Have and Have Not* along these lines.

Unfortunately *A Farewell to Arms*, which contains Hemingway's best single statement on language, receives brief coverage in order to allow for an extended treatment of *For Whom the Bell Tolls*, "his most imaginative novel" and the natural culmination of all the early works and experiments. Wagner's two chapters on this novel are an important contribution, with Michael Reynold's *Hemingway's First War: The Making of A Farewell to Arms* (1976), to the growing awareness that the real origins of Hemingway's fiction are in his literary mentors and not in early experience, traumatic or otherwise. She demonstrates, for example, that *For Whom the Bell Tolls* is the product of invention and imagination composed in parallel configurations of character, chapters, and incidents which reveal a careful structure. Earlier criticism had tended to ignore Hemingway's craft and focus on Spain, war and bullfighting, and other aspects of Hemingway's biography. I was disappointed, however, in Wagner's treatment of *Across the River and Into the Trees*. She ignores his use of humor and parody and neglects to extend her earlier discussion of Hemingway's structure to his obvious use of Dante. Moreover, she makes only brief mention of the last two novels as culminations or possibly failures of Hemingway's earlier craft. More time might have been spent on the last novels in the light of her earlier technical focus and Hemingway's own assessment of that crucial period in Paris which he presented in *A Moveable Feast*.

Less discussion is devoted to Faulkner, but again Wagner's concentration is on the consistent technical development of his work. She begins by dealing primarily with how and where the two authors "touched" each other professionally. She especially notes Faulkner's insistence that "facts and truth don't really have much to do with each other." Significantly, both abandoned formal education after high school and depended on reading and friends for education in both the craft and the content of their works. Wagner's analysis of Faulkner's early writing parallels her consideration of Hemingway's early experiments. Their relation to Eliot and Cezanne suggest many studies to come. Basically she argues that Faulkner's early writing lacks the self-confidence which his later craft solidifies. "The Craft of Fiction", [chapter nine], is a unified reading of Faulkner's major novels introduced by the information that Lubbock's book was one of the few volumes on the aesthetics of fiction in Faulkner's library. Faulkner learned, as did Hemingway, to substitute the single scene for image; character and plot. As a result, Faulkner emerged etched on the Southern landscape because of his confident expansion of crucial scenes. The relation to Hemingway begins to solidify.

Faulkner's larger visions, evident primarily in the novels from 1929 to 1936, resulted from "a decided parallel between the kind of philosophical position he takes and the method of narration he uses. The more stable his view, the more direct and understandable his method."

In her final assessment she champions Faulkner as the better craftsman, but Hemingway runs a close second. Faulkner's primary theme became man's responsibility to other men whereas, for Hemingway, man's responsibility was generally directed toward the self. This is why Faulkner developed an epic talent out of his poetic origins while Hemingway moved in the direction of the lyric. A final note of irony may qualify Wagner's assessment of their respective talents. Although she finds Faulkner the better writer she admits that contemporary tastes seem to favor Hemingway's more succinct prose. In the final analysis she wonders if endurance might not depend on readability. This provocative assessment served as a serious challenge for many readers and critics in the years ahead.

Chapter 1

THE LIBRARY AT FINCA VIGIA

E rnest Hemingway's principal residence from 1938 until his death in 1961 was the *Finca Vigia*, a large, white, hacienda-style villa on thirteen acres of land south of Havana, Cuba. In August 1961, about a month after Hemingway's death, with Cuban-American relations rapidly deteriorating, Mary Hemingway obtained a special permit from the American government and returned to Cuba. She spent almost a month collecting letters and manuscripts from the *Finca Vigia* and from bank vaults in Havana where Hemingway had placed his working manuscripts when he left Cuba, and generally putting the house in order while arrangements were being made for her to "donate" the *Finca* to the Cuban people. When she left on the last American commercial vessel to depart the island before the U.S. embargo went into effect, she had to abandon most of the contents of the house, including the extensive library which she and Hemingway had collected.[1] In the fifteen years since Mrs. Hemingway's departure, little information has been available about the *Finca* and its library.[2]

In October 1976, Joseph Sigman and I attended the Hemingway symposium at the University of Alabama in Tuscaloosa and met Mary Hemingway for the first time, although we had corresponded earlier regarding publication of Hemingway's letters. Her comments on the library at the *Finca* attracted our special attention. After some

1

further correspondence which led to an understanding of mutual concern, Mrs. Hemingway wrote a letter to Fidel Castro asking him to grant permission for us to catalogue the library at the *Finca*. The letter was forwarded to His Excellency, James E. Hyndman, the Canadian Ambassador to Cuba, for personal delivery to Dr. Castro. After contacting the Cuban embassy in Ottawa and the External Affairs Department of the Canadian government, trying for three days to complete a telephone call to Havana (one morning we were simply told Havana was not answering), and sending letters and cablegrams which elicited a meager response, we decided to go to Havana and find out for ourselves what arrangements we could make. In November. 1979, the Arts Research Committee of McMaster University approved our plans and awarded us a research grant to make a preliminary analysis of the library in Cuba. On 30 December we arrived at the splendid new Hotel Marazul with the usual batch of Canadian tourists and began our attack from closer quarters. On the following day, the Canadian Embassy in Havana delivered to us a letter from the Cuban Ministry of Culture instructing Cuban officials to facilitate our research. Mrs. Hemingway's letter had apparently been delivered and was favourably received.

After a weekend on the Marazul beach, we were able to meet with Gladys Rodriguez, a representative of the Ministry of Culture, and Marta Arjona, Director of Museums and Monuments for all of Cuba. As a result of this meeting we were provided with a car, a driver, and a guide/translator and were given access to the *Finca*. During our all-too-brief visits, we were shown about the house and grounds and permitted to photograph the grounds as well as the exteriors and interiors of the buildings. Also, we were able to examine the books, to photograph marginalia and dedications, and to record information about the library on a tape recorder. Time limitations and a renovation project prevented us from examining the entire library, but we did take systematic records in a number of rooms in order to provide a statistical foundation for further study and analysis. We were prevented from descending the stirs in the kitchen which led to the basement.

On 6 January we met again with Mrs. Arjona and were able to interview her at some length about the *Finca*. After our return to

Canada, we visited Mary Hemingway in her apartment in New York City and had a lengthy discussion with her about the *Finca* and its library. We presented our assessment of the condition of the books, and we outlined what proposals we made to the Cuban and Canadian governments for the preservation of the library. Our concerns have not been addressed and focus has now turned to the some 3,000 items found stored in the basement which because of our focus on the books, we had not been permitted to see.

After the Revolution, the Cuban government decided that Hemingway's home should be preserved as a museum. A minimum amount of work was done to preserve and restore the house, and about a year after Mrs. Hemingway left the *Finca*, public access to the grounds was granted to the public. It fell under the general authority of the Ministry of Culture and it is still administered by the director of all Cuban museums and monuments. A staff of about twenty people has been assigned to the *Finca*.. We were told that some 40,000 people visit the *Finca* every year. In the last few years arrangements have been made to admit scholars and produce a duplicate record of the remaining fragments which will also be available to scholars at the Kennedy Library.

About 40% of these visitors are Cuban students who go there on school visits. One morning when we were there, about 100 Cuban schoolchildren in their blue uniforms visited. Two busloads of tourists, including Japanese and Eastern Europeans, were also there. It seemed safe to conclude that the *Finca Vigia* was both a national monument and a major tourist attraction.

At the present time tourists are not allowed into the house. They may walk freely around the grounds to view the swimming pool and the exteriors of the various buildings. Many of the large windows in the house are left open so that visitors may look into the rooms. Since the house has only one main floor and there are many windows, visitors are able to obtain a good view of the interior. Security is excellent at present, and there are attendants outside the house and in each room when visitors are present. A visitor is able to get a very good picture of the estate, but permission to actually enter the house is difficult to obtain and is usually given only to visiting dignitaries. We were told that we were the first scholars to be given access to the books.

There are three buildings on the estate. Dominating the top of the hill is the *Finca* itself, its back windows commanding a magnificent view over the hills to Havana. Smog reduces the view today. The villa contains seven rooms: front sitting room, library, dining room, Hemingway's bedroom/study, Mary Hemingway's bedroom, guest room (the Venetian room), and kitchen. It is a sizeable, but not at all huge building. Secondly, there is the tower which Mrs. Hemingway built in order to get the cats out of the house at night and to give Hemingway a quiet place to work away from cooking and cleaning noises. (In fact, he rarely used it for writing.) The tower stands to the left of the main house at the rear. The first floor of the tower has been converted into a laundry room, the second serves as the administrative office of the museum while on the third floor are displayed hunting equipment, guns, a rack of swords, and an assortment of hunting footgear. In Hemingway's time it was simply a luggage room. The fourth and top floor is the intended writing studio. It contains a desk and about 400 volumes of the library in two book cases. Also, there is the telescope which Mrs. Hemingway sometimes transported to the roof of the tower in order to study the stars. The tower rises above the surrounding vegetation, permitting almost a 360 degree view of the horizon from the fourth floor and roof. The third building on the estate is the *casita*—the little house—built as a guest house and now functioning as a lounge for the staff and as a storage and work area. Cats still roam.

As the efforts put into the operation and maintenance of the *Finca* indicate, Hemingway is still highly regarded in Cuba. Cuban schoolchildren are taken to the *Finca* just as they are to the Museum of the Revolution. To a considerable degree, Hemingway seems to be thought of as a local hero and almost a Cuban writer.[3] As Mrs. Arjona explained to us, he is well-remembered. He knew many Cubans; he wrote about Cuba and chose to make it his home for over twenty years. *The Old Man and The Sea* is popular because it concerns a Cuban fisherman, and *For Whom The Bell Tolls* is also highly thought of in Cuba as in other Communist countries. Mrs. Arjona told us that Fidel Castro admires it for its portrayal of guerilla warfare"[4] Hemingway's sympathy for the Loyalist side in the Spanish Civil War suggests to Cubans that he would have looked with favor on the new Cuba. As Mrs. Arjona said to us, "If Hemingway were alive today, he would be very interested in what was happening in Cuba. He would never have been an enemy of the Cuban people."

As a result of these feelings, not only the *Finca* but other sites associated with Hemingway are carefully preserved. In Mrs. Arjona's words, "His presence is still felt in many parts of Havana." Before Martha Gellhorn found the *Finca* and talked him into buying it, Hemingway lived in a room in the Ambos Mundos Hotel in downtown Havana.[5] This hotel, now nationalized, belongs to the Ministry of Education and serves as a residence for Cuban educators visiting the capital. However, Hemingway's room (#511) has been set aside. Guests may not use it, but like the *Finca*, it may be visited by tourists. Similarly, the two Havana bars most associated with Hemingway, the *Floridita* and the *Bodequita*, are still open for business and retain Hemingway associations. Employees in both recalled Hemingway and were happy to talk about him.

The *Finca Vigia*, however, remains the chief memorial to Hemingway and the Cuban government has taken considerable care to preserve it. In general, the house is maintained in good condition and while we were there, restoration was under way on the right wing, which contains Mrs. Hemingway's bedroom. The roots of the huge Cieba tree no longer disrupt the floor of the *Finca* as they did in Hemingway's time.[6] The dining room table is set with the lovely glassware that Mrs. Hemingway designed and had made in Venice. Hemingway's favorite chair still stands in the front room with the same cover visible in old photographs. The gin and tonic fixings stand ready for use. The extensive record collection from which Hemingway could select his favorite program of Mozart mixed with Fats Waller[7] dominates one entire end of the front room. The typewriter and the writing board are still on the bookcase in Hemingway's bedroom where he worked, standing up beside his bed. On a table beside the bed are Hemingway's glasses. We were told that the animal heads decorating the walls are one of the chief preservation problems since the hides deteriorate rapidly in the tropical climate.

The chief difference between the *Finca* as it now exists and as it was when the Hemingways lived there is the absence of the small but impressive collection of modernist paintings which the Hemingways owned-a Miró, five André Massons, a Braque, two Juan Gris, several Roberto Domingo bullfight paintings and a superb Paul Klee.[8] Miró's "The Farm" was fortunately sent to an exhibition at the Museum of Modern Art in Washington while Hemingway was still in Cuba. The Braque was stolen by thieves posing as government "art surveyors" while Mrs. Hemingway was in the United States during Hemingway's stay in hospital. Mrs. Hemingway persuaded Castro to allow her to remove the remaining paintings in 1961.[9] She decided, however, to leave the Domingos behind.

The house can fairly be said to be filled with books. There are bookcases in every room (including Hemingway's bathroom) except the kitchen and dining room, in the tower, and the *casita* as well. We estimated there were about 7,000 books although our final tally was considerably higher since we found his books in other locations. In general, the condition of the books is good. They are subject, however, to the deterioration natural in a hot, humid climate. There was no dehumidifying equipment anywhere in the *Finca* and many of the books (in the front room, for example) were literally soaking with water. According to Mrs. Arjona, efforts to preserve the books have been limited to fumigation. She informed us that the books are removed from the *Finca* once a year and taken to the National Museum in Havana for treatment. We found this difficult to reconcile with the condition of the library as we observed it

We found that some of the books have suffered serious worm damage. This, however, appears to be confined to the older books, some of which were in Hemingway's possession for forty years before his death. Some of the older paper was deteriorating and a great deal of it had turned yellow. This is particularly true, as one would expect, of the poor quality paper in the old paperbound French and Spanish books. The scope of the library is extensive in terms of both chronology and subject matter.[10] Chronologically speaking, Hemingway acquired the books in the Finca over a range of about forty years. A large number of American novels were purchased in the 50s. A Spanish novel bears the words "Madrid, 1921" on the flyleaf. In terms of subject matter, the books reflect the wide range of Hemingway's interests. According to Mrs. Hemingway, he read omnivorously, and the library testifies to this. There are history books (on the American and Spanish Civil Wars and World War II especially), guide and travel books, a vast amount of fiction—in English, French, and Spanish—poetry, books on art, wildlife, literary criticism, politics, military tactics, bullfighting, sports, exploration, and various technical subjects. Also there are runs of periodicals, such as *The Partisan Review*, and editions of Hemingway's works in many languages, including Japanese and Russian. The books appeared to us to be in no particular order whatsoever. As the rest of the chapters in this book demonstrate, many references to the library inform his correspondence.

Our visit to the *Finca* made it clear to us that efforts should be made to preserve the library. After evaluating our investigatory trip and consulting with bibliographical and computer specialists at McMaster University, we developed a project with two basic goals. The first goal was to make a permanent record of the library. It seems unlikely that the Cuban Ministry of Culture will move the books in the foreseeable future. Suggestions about the possibility of moving the books to the *Biblioteca Nacional Jose Marti* or the *Museo Nacional* were met with firm rejections. Moreover, even if the books were moved at this point, they would continue to deteriorate. Accordingly, we proposed to the Cuban authorities that we microfilm the title pages and versos of each volume and all inscriptions, dedications, marginalia, and under-lining. This microfilm would be available at Mills Memorial Library at McMaster, at some as yet undesignated repository in Cuba, and possibly the John F Kennedy Library in Boston. This suggestion is now being continued by a grant from the Rockefeller Foundation, but the digital material will be available at the Kennedy Library and the soon to be completed library attached to the *Finca*. No plans to record dedications or marginalia in Hemingway's books have been announced.

Our second goal was the publication of a catalogue. The completion of this project was accomplished by the publication of *Hemingway's Library: A Composite Record* (1981). This present volume provides

7

a context for that publication which is now available on line at the John F. Kennedy Library in Boston, MA. [Google: "Hemingway's Library"]

Mary Hemingway later confirmed confusion in the library. "We were terribly haphazard about the library .... We had absolutely no organization. I would not know where to go, for example, for the dictionaries or the atlases or H. L. Mencken [that]was down there on the left-hand side in the library."[11] In 1955, Hemingway wrote Fraser Drew, a former teacher of mine, that the once orderly library had suffered hurricanes, moves, and re-organizations, and that on one occasion his boys rearranged the books according to size and color.[12]

During informal conversation at the Hemingway symposium at the University of Alabama in October 1976, Mrs. Hemingway had not only suggested that some surprises might be found in the library, but that a considerable amount of under-lining and commentary would also be found. Since time limitations required that most of our recorded survey be conducted without paging through the books, the extent of marginalia remains difficult to estimate. Suffice it to say that there was a considerable amount. We found, for example, a provocative comment in Colin Wilson's *The Outsider*, a signed marginal comment arguing with O'Faolain in *The Vanishing Hero: The Hero in the Modern Novel*, and Hemingway's corrections added to one of his stories in a casually displayed copy of *Esquire*. Thomas Mann's *The Magic Mountain* had been used as a fishing log. Hemingway had a habit of checking items in the table of contents and also a personal system of check marks and under-linings in the text. We found a number of works, particularly volumes of poetry, marked in this fashion. One un-namable book contained the remark "This writer is full of shit [signed] EH."

In general the library demonstrates the extraordinary range of Hemingway's reading and his scholarly cast of mind, especially in the later years. It is interesting to compare the *Finca's* collection of some 7000 volumes with the library of "close to 1200 volumes" that Faulkner collected[13] at his home in Mississippi. Such a comparison lends support to the contemporary trend in Hemingway criticism, readily visible in Michael Reynolds's book which sees the novels less as autobiographical accounts of Hemingway's experience than as intellectually shaped works that owe a great deal to Hemingway's reading and his sense of literary content and style.[14] Some discussion of Hemingway's interest in poetry and art may assist in understanding Hemingway's dependence on his library.

Chapter 2

POETRY AND ART IN
HEMINGWAY'S LIBRARY

R ather than reproduce the enormous inventory of the books and the lengthy introduction to Hemingway's literary habits which are now conveniently available on line at the John F Kennedy library [Google: "Hemingway's Library"] it seems more appropriate to focus attention on two aspects of the library which demonstrate the depth and breadth of Hemingway's interest and his dependence on literary texts. This discussion, published originally in Japan, is an attempt to illustrate the importance of reading to Hemingway's style. The recent unacknowledged editing of the manuscript of *The Garden of Eden*, the unexplained omission of 5/6 of Hemingway's letters from Carlos Baker's edition of *Ernest Hemingway: Selected Letters, 1917—1961*,[1] the curious manipulation during the editing of *A Moveable Feast* and the Hemingway Foundation's refusal to permit the publication of the complete correspondence between Hemingway and Malcolm Cowley raise serious questions about the editing of Hemingway's manuscripts. These irregularities are particularly unsettling when they affect what Hemingway recorded about his theory of fiction and combine to promote an autobiographical fallacy that is finally being subjected to considerable scrutiny. A case in point is the elimination of a relatively long fragment of the manuscript of *A Moveable Feast,* a revised edition of which has recently been published. Another aspect of the library that is generally unacknowledged, but which reveals that "other" Hemingway was his dependence on volumes of poetry.

When Hemingway wrote to Bernard Berenson in 1954 that he felt "the obligation to invent truer than things can be true"[2] he was describing a theory of fiction that was far more rigorous than the ambiguous last paragraph of the Preface to *A Moveable Feast*: "If the reader prefers, this book may be regarded as fiction, but there is always the chance that such a book of fiction may throw some light on what has been written as fact."[3] More vital than this vague disclaimer is the omission of an entire section of the manuscript of *A Moveable Feast* in which Hemingway discusses the theory and purpose of his fiction. He wants to achieve a fiction that is "real beyond any reality," Since the passage was type-written with little change from the original holograph, Hemingway obviously intended to include it in successive drafts of the manuscript of *A Moveable Feast*. Why it was omitted is puzzling because the passage reveals several of Hemingway's reasons for writing his reminiscences of Paris and helps to clarify several other passages in the memoir which relate directly to his theory of fiction. (pp. 75, 91, 156, 159, 173, for example) Fortunately it is short enough to be included here in its entirety.

> When you first start writing stories in the first person if the stories are made so real that people believe them the people reading them nearly always think the stories really happened to you. That is natural because while you were making them up you had to make them happen to the person who was telling them. If you do this successfully enough you make the person who is reading them believe that the things happened to him too. If you can do this you are beginning to get what you are trying for which is to make the story so real beyond any reality that it will become a part of the readers [sic] experience and a part of his memory. There must be things that he did not notice when he read the story of the novel which without his knowing it, enter into his memory and experience so that they are a part of his life. This is not easy to do.

What is, if not easy, almost always possible to do is for members of the private detective (private eye) school of literary criticism to prove that the writer of fiction written in the first person could not possibly have done everything that the narrator did or, perhaps, not even any of it. What importance this has or what it proves except the the [sic] writer is not devoid of imagination or the power of invention, I have never understood.

In the early days writing in Paris I would invent not only from my own experiences but from the experiences and knowledge of all my friends and all the people I had known or met since I could remember who were not writers. I was very lucky always, that my best friends were not writers and to have known many intelligent people who were articulate. In Italy when I was at the war there for one thing that I had seen or that had happened to me [sic] I knew many hundreds of things that had happened to other people who had been in the war in all of its phases. My own small experiences gave me a touchstone by which I could tell whether stories were true or false and being wounded was a (sort of) pass word. After the war I spent much time in the 19th ward and other Italian quarters in Chicago with an Italian friend I had made while in hospital in Milano. He was a young officer then and had been severely wounded many times. He had gone from Seattle I think to Italy to visit family there and had volunteered when Italy came into the war. We were very good friends and he was a wonderful story teller.

In Italy too I had known many people in the British army and in their ambulance service. Much that I later invented from in writing I learned from them. My best friend for many years was a young British professional soldier who had gone from Sandhurst to Mons in 1914 and who had served with troops until the end of the war in 1918."[4]

This passage, omitted from *A Moveable Feast*, and published here for the first time[5] especially when taken in the context of some similar statements in unpublished letters emphasizes that Hemingway's style was the product of conscious creative invention and not the result of some casual or calculated application of reportorial skills to experience. At least three distinct aspects of Hemingway's theory of fiction are developed in the passage: 1) Fiction must give the reader a real experience; 2) truth in fiction depends primarily on invention rather than fidelity to actual events and experience; and 3) Hemingway's use of the first person is a calculated dimension of invention and not a matter of recording personal experience.

I

Hemingway believed that fiction was capable of capturing the truth of a situation more accurately than any straight-forward reporting. When he wrote to Bernard Berenson that he felt "the obligation to invent truer than things can be true," he was recording the compulsion behind his career. Truth is not a factual record on which fiction can be based, but truth is a dimension of fiction beyond facts. In addition to the unpublished fragment quoted above, at least seven short portions of the manuscript[6] on the fictional dimension and intent of *A Moveable Feast* were eliminated from the published version. These seven fragments of the manuscript insist that "the book is fiction" and support Hemingway's contention that fiction is "realer than real." The editor's statement in the "Preface" reaffirms the conventional assumption that fiction and reality tend to blend together and that it is difficult to detect where one leaves off and the other begins. Hemingway assumed such blending, but he was determined to keep his own experience separate from what he had invented. Any biographer, Hemingway argued, writing while he himself was still alive, would tend to blend actual experience and fiction in a biography. Readers of Baker, Fenton, Young, Donaldson, Meyers and Brenner, to mention only a few, are now well aware of what

Hemingway feared during his lifetime. His experience, Hemingway felt, was his personal reservoir and he did not want anyone to tamper with it. More importantly, it was his private experience. His fiction was something else. Facts always remained facts. There was nothing necessarily real about facts, especially when the facts were a part of the past. The "truth" in the event was beyond the event and could best be revealed in fiction. The "feast" was a metaphor for fiction; the Paris of history as actual place was for impressionists. How a higher dimension could be achieved is often the real subject matter of *A Moveable Feast*.

There has always been a suggestion in the criticism that Hemingway had cleverly disguised the facts and identities of the sources of some of his fiction, and that he was frequently disguising his own experiences or protecting the privacy of friends. The fragment quoted clearly establishes the actual intent. The purpose was not to disguise or protect, but to reveal. He wanted to recall and reveal a reality beyond the facts, to invent a reality that captured the essence which was beyond actuality. In short what Hemingway's fiction involves is not an attempt to help the reader to experience what it was like to be in Paris in the old days. Hemingway wanted his fiction to provide an authentic personal experience for the reader. Hemingway wanted the reader of his prose to experience the solidity of his prose just as thoroughly and as intimately as anyone could experience the actual smells and cobble stones of Paris. Hemingway achieved this actuality by the introduction of "things." In the quoted fragment Hemingway describes how he achieved this effect:

> "There must be things that he [the reader] did
> not notice when he read the story of the novel which
> without his knowing it, enter into his memory and
> experience so that they are a part of his life."

In other words, the reader was supposed to encounter the fiction as a dimension of his own experience—not as a dimension of Hemingway's experience. Encountering the fiction was no different from encountering a fallen tree in the forest or a rock in the foreground of a Cezanne painting or an apple in a still life composition. Once encountered, the apple remains a matter of the viewer's experience.

Encountering "things," Hemingway here suggests, is as important as the things that are sometimes left out. The "iceberg" theory was only part of what Hemingway understood about invention. When Hemingway refers to the creation and insertion of things he reveals one method by which the tip of the iceberg showing above water was constructed. We have heard a great deal about "the thing left out"; here Hemingway is writing about what was put in. To register the total reality of a scene on the reader and at the same time produce a Cezanne-like presence or image which would remain with the reader, Hemingway frequently inserted "things" into the narrative. In the following passage from "*An Alpine Idyll*" we can see "things" that are incorporated, as carefully as Cezanne arranged skulls, bottles and apples in a still-life. As John and the narrator talk of doing something "too long" the narrator records:

> The sun came through the open window and shone through the beer bottles on the table. The bottles were half full. There was a little froth on the beer in the bottles, not much because it was very cold. It collared up when you poured it into the tall glasses. I looked out of the open window at the white road. The trees beside the road were dusty. Beyond was a green field and a stream. There were trees along the stream and a mill with a water wheel. Through the open side of the mill I saw a long log and a saw in it rising and falling. No one seemed to be tending it. There were four crows walking in the green field. One crow sat in a tree watching. Outside on the porch the cook got off his chair and passed into the hall that led back into the kitchen. Inside, the sunlight shone through the empty glasses on the table. John was leaning forward with his head on his arms.[7]

Not only does the passage provide specific "things" for the reader to experience and, thus, participate in John's experience, but the stark simplicity and reality of the images prefigure the final grotesque scene of the story. The bizarre revelation of the ending is only another "thing" in the series of images which go to make up the story and which the reader has already experienced. Once the reader has participated in seeing the slant of light coming through the beer bottles, he cannot stand apart when the images turn grotesque. The style traps the reader into participating in the grotesque ending. "The "truth" of the ending is rendered more horrible because of the earlier things—the open window, the beer bottles, the froth, the tall glasses, the white road, the green field, the stream, the trees, the mill with a water wheel, a long log, four crows—that have entered the consciousness of the reader.

The word in *A Moveable Feast* that reveals Hemingway's technique for the introduction of "things" is "make": "I had started to break down all my writing and get rid of all facility and try to make instead of describe"[8] This reveals that Hemingway was not trying in his early fiction to help the reader to live vicariously in Paris, Upper Michigan or Spain. He was trying to "make" a composition, the experience of which would be important for its own sake. A few years earlier in the context of a discussion on Cezanne and other painters, Hemingway had used the same expression in a description of his technique:

> I can make a landscape like Mr. Paul Cezanne. I walked through the Luxembourg Museum a thousand times with an empty gut, and I am pretty sure that if Mr. Paul was around, he would like the way I make them and be happy that I learned it from him.[9]

This is not merely another naturalistic fidelity to actuality, but a creation out of language for the purpose of establishing a fictional encounter in a dimension not considered before Hemingway.

Just as Cezanne sought to reveal the essence of *Mt. Ste. Victoire* and what was permanent in nature by emphasizing the basic geometry of the scene, so Hemingway sought the essence of a scene in an image of sharp angles, juxtaposed contrasts, distortions of language, distorted bodies, and variations in the diction and dialects of the English language. The angles of the horses' broken legs in Smyrna haunt not only Hemingway but anyone who has experienced these images of war by reading his vignettes or stories. The images are in fiction, not in history, geography or experience. The landscape of *In Our Time* is strewn with things, abrupt images, puzzling juxtapositions and real objects that ever after trouble the observant reader. One way to explain this troubled response to stark juxtaposition is to discuss "the things left out."[10] What the manuscript contained and what the omitted fragment emphasizes is a concern for what Ernest Hemingway deliberately put in.

Hemingway revealed what he "put in" by his revelation in *A Moveable Feast* that he was trying "to make instead of describe" and that he could "make a scene" like Paul Cezanne. He defined what he meant by the word "make" in his correspondence with Bernard Berenson. What he was trying to do, he explained, was "to move people emotionally with the landscape without being descriptive."[11]() To Malcolm Cowley, Hemingway explained his technique by insisting that when a writer writes, he should, "make something so that it will really happen to the reader; be made (not described); so that afterwards the reader will have had the experience, not seen it or heard about it"[12] This was why, Hemingway admitted, writing got harder and harder to do. We now know that one of the reasons it got harder was that he saw his work more in the context of Cezanne's painting than in the context of traditional fiction. Like Cezanne, Hemingway wanted to make something new out of a scene rather than present character, setting, plot and resolution in a conventional way. After the successes of nineteenth century fiction, it was easy, perhaps, to get the reader to participate in the hero's experience. After World War I, however, Hemingway was faced with the problem of having the reader experience a despair which was best portrayed by "making" a scene. Landscape, scene and imagery become more important than experience. *A Farewell to Arms* and *The Sun Also Rises* are novels about place—things—rather than novels of character, love and the excitement of war and its aftermath. Goya and Cezanne were his teachers, but his readers were not used to "seeing" fiction. This was why he had to "make" a scene, not describe it. If the reader could experience the scene as Hemingway made it, perhaps he could also experience what Frederick Henry or Nick felt as they looked at what was left of Wordsworth's "steep and lofty cliffs," Thoreau's woods, and Arnold's "darkling plain."

Hemingway considered his novels and short stories new versions of his original intent in the same way Cezanne considered yet another version of *Mont Ste. Victoire* as another attempt at revealing the reality of the mountain's natural permanent geometric solidity. In the perceptively titled chapter of *A Moveable Feast*, "Birth of a New School," Hemingway indicated that when he was working well, he "could make the country so that you could walk into it through the timber to come out into the clearing and work up onto the high ground and see the hills beyond the arm of the lake."[13] On another occasion he explained to Berenson: "I know how to make country so that you, when you wish, can walk into it."[14] Accurate description was not the purpose. Hemingway wanted his reader to encounter the elements of the short story or the vignette just as Cezanne wanted to force a new experience or perception of *Mont. Ste. Victoire* or an apple, or his agent, on the viewer. Left behind is the early impressionism of Monet, Renoir and perhaps Debussy and T. S. Eliot. What remains is the determination of the post impressionists like Gauguin, Van Gogh and Cezanne to create a new encounter (as a monument in a museum, Cezanne insisted). What Hemingway shared with these men was a determination that the audience should experience the created experience, not merely share in Hemingway's impression of an earlier experience. As Hemingway admitted, "This was not easy to do."

As early as 1924 Hemingway explained his method to Edward O'Brien:

> What I've been doing is trying to do country so you don't remember the words after you read it but actually have the Country. It is hard because to do it you have to see the country all complete all the time you write and not just have a romantic feeling about it. It is swell fun.[15]

This was "swell fun" because, and Hemingway was well aware of it, this was a new fiction. William Carlos Williams would have understood that "so much depends/upon" Hemingway's desire to "do country."

II

The second element of Hemingway's style emphasized in the omitted fragment is his notion of "invention."[16] Knowledge, the source of invention, is a different commodity than fact. Facts are identified with events and experience. This distinction is best understood in the language of Henry James.[17] Hemingway was surely echoing James's "The Art of Fiction" when he wrote to Berenson, "A writer should know too much."[18] Out of "too much" knowledge the writer can select and invent as necessary. In an exchange over what Hemingway knew about the various fishes mentioned in *The Old Man and the Sea*, he wrote to Malcolm Cowley, "Ideally a man should know everything"[19] Experience was crucial insofar as it produced knowledge from which the writer could invent. Experience alone was not sufficient for fiction. James had insisted that the young writer should try to be one on whom nothing was lost. Unless experience was supported by knowledge—of Caribbean fishes, for example—it was of little use to the writer.[20] Hemingway recognized a distinct relationship between experience, knowledge and invention. Making it "realer than real" was a process of invention, not recording experience itself. Hemingway wrote to Berenson:

> Writers of fiction are only super-liars who if they know enough and are disciplined can make their lies truer than the truth...When you have the knowledge to lie out of. That is all a writer of fiction is.[21]

In another fragment in the Kennedy Library, Hemingway expands on the relationship between lying and inventing:

> "It is not un-natural that the best writers are liars, A major part of their trade is to lie or invent and they will lie when they are drunk, or to themselves, or to strangers. They often lie unconsciously and then remember their lies with deep remorse. If they knew all other writers were liars too it would cheer them .... Lying when drinking is a good exercise for their powers of invention and is very helpful in the making up of a story. It is no more wicked or reprehensible in a writer than ... it is to have strange and marvelous experiences in ... dreams. Lying to themselves is

harmful but this is cleansed away by the writing of a true book which in its invention is truer than any true thing that ever happened."[22]

Truth, as always, is the result of invention, not fidelity to details. The important distinction was that truth and experience were realms apart. Lying, invention or the creation of fiction were all part of the same process intended to create a reality beyond the real, a truth beyond the truth. This is what Nick means by "making it up":

> Writing about anything actual was bad. It always killed it. The only writing that was any good was what you made up, what you imagined. That made everything come true .... Everything good he'd ever written he'd made up. None of it had ever happened. Other things had happened. Better things, maybe. That was what the family couldn't understand. They thought it was all experience.[23]

Making it up, lying, writing fiction are all the same and none of this has much to do with autobiography-how it was, or what had actually happened.

Hemingway wrote to Berenson about how the act of invention creates a certain detachment or objectivity that leads to the words becoming experience or encounters themselves:

> It always reads to me, then, when it's very good as though I must have stolen it from somebody else and then I think and remember that nobody else knew about it and that it never really happened and so I must have invented it and I feel very happy.[24]

Here the invented text is as real as any other experience. And so we are back to Hemingway's old admiration for Tolstoy—the master who could "invent from knowledge."[25] Hemingway greatly admired Tolstoy's description of the battle of Borodino in *War and Peace*, but he knew that Tolstoy had invented the entire description of the battle from the experience he had at Sevastopol and later reading about the battle of Borodino. Tolstoy had not been at Borodino and had lied, invented, or made the whole thing up.[26] Tolstoy's ability to invent was never far from Hemingway's mind.

"Inventing" out of knowledge resulted in a different reality than the conventional realism proposed by those who celebrate Hemingway's superb reportorial skills combined with extraordinary experience. Knowledge, not experience, was the source of invention. Hemingway's interest in boxing was a good example of the knowledge he sought as a source of invention. The false myth has it that boxing demonstrated Hemingway's unlettered talent and supported the "dumb-ox" school of Hemingway criticism. Patiently Hemingway tried to explain the relationship of boxing to writing to Charles A. Fenton, who was begging Hemingway in the early 1950's for permission to publish a biography. From the exasperated tone of the letter, one suspects Hemingway had little hope of succeeding:

> ...For instance I knew I always received many strong sensations when I went into the gym to train and work out with boxers. I didn't know what the things were that made them so. I would think that I was wrapping my hands and remember. First, there was the smell of wintergreen in the liniment, where guys were being rubbed. Then there were the different sweat smells and the smell of the crowd that paid two bits in to watch the work outs. And the smell of the individual people like Eddie McGurkey, Tommy Gibbons, Johnny Wilson, Jack Dillon Grebb, and others. Then the noise of the different bags being worked on. Then the sniffing that tightens the gut that boxers make as they shadow box. Then the noise of the resin crunching underfoot in the corner as you scuffle your shoes on it and the squeak it made against the canvas.
>
> When I would get back from the gym I would write them down. The same with baseball. That could be the way a fielder threw his glove without looking where it landed as he trotted in.

21

Football I knew too much about and it did not interest me really, and I have never written a lot about it.

Bullfighting I learned just like you would learn navigation, if you had to make up your own tables. I did that for discipline.[27]

In this unpublished excerpt from of a letter to Fenton, there is a hardness, a discipline, and a passionate pursuit of craft recorded that goes beyond the usual casual biographical assumptions. Hemingway's passion for knowledge which grew out of his programs for self-control and self-discipline depict a writer far beyond a recording journalist. What is interesting to note is that the reviewers and critics who were emotionally unable to accept a boisterous writer who was interested in boxing and bull-fighting, tended to ignore the fact that the real craft of the man was writing. Mastering the details of a sport or mapping the coast of Cuba was only a means of self-discipline which could lead to self-control and specific knowledge. Just as Melville studied the business of whaling, Hemingway studied the details of bullfighting, boxing, and marlin fishing. The constant was inventing a new reality—writing fiction.

III

The third stylistic commentary in the omitted fragment concerns Hemingway's use of the first-person narrator in such a way so as "to make things happen to the person telling them." Learning to write in the first person, was for Hemingway part of the process of invention. It was not a way of turning his experience into fiction. Hemingway explained to Charles Atkins why he had worked at learning the use of the first person:

"When I wrote the first two novels I had not learned to write in the third person. The first person gives you great intimacy."[28] It is now a historical fact that "the great intimacy" which Hemingway "invented" for the purpose of reality resulted in a critical assumption that Hemingway was fictionalizing his own experience. Beneath Hemingway's objections to these facile assertions was the assumption that any biographer would confuse his mother lode of experience. Still deeper in Hemingway's mind lay an abiding insult to his power of invention.

Hemingway, recognized the insult, as paragraph two of the fragment reveals. Many critics implied that Hemingway didn't have enough imagination to "invent." On the other hand, some critics insist on making biographical assumptions on the basis of events recorded in fiction. This confusion between what had actually happened and what Hemingway had invented was what particularly troubled Hemingway. Fenton was only the first of the many critics who infuriated Hemingway.[29] According to Hemingway, Fenton had recorded the details of much of his life, but the significance of the details and their relation to his writing eluded him. Hemingway would never agree with Fenton that the "principal instrument of his literary apprenticeship was journalism."[30] The principal instrument was invention.

And by inventing the fiction, that was "realer than real, truer than true" Hemingway forced the reader to encounter a new reality. Hemingway's language, itself, became the place to live in the post World War I scene. Meaning, after the folly and carnage of the war became a dimension of language. Hemingway's life-long search for a place of natural peace was beginning to take shape along the lines suggested by Pound. Meaning only found a metaphor in the bull ring, the Serengeti or the Gulf Stream. Truth, as Pound had insisted was only found in language. Once Hemingway's words were encountered in the world, the world was a new place. It was a new place: "the great good place," James called it, beyond "madness, surrender, collapse."[31] James's analysis of place had foreshadowed the loss of place, rootlessness and amorality portrayed in the "lost generation." Invented narratives were realer than real and truer than true because they were beyond experience. Perhaps this was the fifth dimension that Hemingway was seeking.

Hemingway's words achieved a truth or reality beyond facts. They represented an actuality in fiction that was its own testament, its own reality beyond the real, a truth beyond the ordinary facts and events. As this fragment omitted from *A Moveable Feast* illustrates, Hemingway was a skilled craftsman who carefully constructed his prose to achieve a reality which was not a dimension of his biography. It was a reality that was a part of the new century. To have not read Hemingway became a sign of inexperience. Perhaps it still is.

This is the most unsettling fact about the posthumous publications. The unidentified editor calmly cut out sections of Hemingway's manuscript in accordance, with facile assumptions about the young journalist described by Baker, Young and Fenton, still in his/her mind. The development of a style that owed more to Cezanne and Goya, to Stendhal and James than it did to Oak Park, Kansas City, Toronto, Upper Michigan, Spain and Italy requires an understanding that has enormous editorial implications for the editing of the manuscripts which have appeared since Hemingway's death. The omission of the "When you first start writing stories..." fragment of *A Moveable Feast* suggests that the editors of these posthumous texts do not really understand Hemingway's creativity and inventiveness.[32] Hemingway's style was "realer than real, truer than true" because Hemingway made it that way. He made fiction that had a dimension beyond the ordinary and far from his own biography. He invented a poetry that read and looked like prose.[33] Wallace Stevens had detected it very early when he noted that Hemingway was "the most significant of living poets," because his fiction revealed "EXTAORDINARY ACTUALITY".[34]

At the symposium in Alabama, Mary Hemingway had suggested her and Hemingway's poetic interest, but the extent of Hemingway's interest and the dependence on poetry was not expanded. Wallace Stevens had intuitively realized the pattern. Visiting *Hemingway's Library* on line at the Kennedy Library reveals an abiding interest of this lonely writer in Cuba. In his edition of *88 Poems by Ernest Hemingway*[35] Nicholas Gerogiannis notes that although Hemingway, like Joyce, Faulkner, and Fitzgerald, "composed a certain amount of verse while he was becoming an established fiction writer," he also "continued to experiment with poetry after he had achieved literary fame." Hemingway's interest in poetry was not limited, however, to writing a small amount of verse at various times. He was also throughout his life a reader of poetry. Our complete bibliography of Hemingway's library, which was published by Garland Press in 1981, lists 229 volumes of poetry. Hemingway read poetry in

French, Spanish, and Italian as well as in English, and the poetry volumes in his library are remarkably diverse, ranging from W. H. Auden's *Oxford Book of Light Verse* and Robert Bridge's edition of the poems of Gerard Manley Hopkins to Lamartine's *Meditations Poetique* and including exotic items such as a Spanish translation of Shelley's *Adonais*. I will focus primarily on four poets, two from the 20th Century and two from the 19th Century, in whom, I believe, Hemingway maintained a serious interest over a long period of time. I will also include a number of related figures.

Hemingway's admiration for Ezra Pound is well-known, and it is not surprising, therefore, that there are more volumes by Pound in Hemingway's library than by any other poet. These volumes range chronologically from a 1916 *Gaudier-Brzeska* to a 1958 *Pavannes and Divagations*; and so it is clear that Hemingway's interest in the work of his old mentor never waned. The following is a complete list of the volumes of Pound's poetry in Hemingway's possession:

A fume spento, 1908-1958. A cura di Vanni Scheiwiller. Milan: Antonini, 1958.

Cantos 91, 96. Brani tradotti da Enzo Siciliano. Genoa: 1958.

A Draft of XVI Cantos of Ezra Pound for the Beginning of a Poem of Some Length. Now first made into a book with initials by Henry Strater. Paris: Three Mountains, 1925.

A Draft of xxx Cantos. New York: Farrar & Rinehart, 1933.

Lustra. [Edition unknown.] [36]

Personae: The Collected Poems, Including Ripostes, Lustra, Homage to Sextus Propertius, H. S. Mauberfey. New York: Boni & Liveright, 1926.

Selected Poems. Edited with an introduction by T. S. Eliot. London: Faber & Gwyer, 1928.

The Translations of Ezra Pound. Introduction by Hugh Kenner. New York: New Directions, n.d.

Umbra: The Early Poems of Ezra Pound, All that He Now Wishes to Keep in Circulation from "Personae", Exultations", Ripostes", etc. With translations from Guido Cavalcanti and Arnaut Daniel, and poems by the late T. E. Hulme. London: Elkin Mathews, 1920.

In addition to these volumes, Hemingway owned the following anthology, which contains six poems by Pound as well as poems by other modernists such as Joyce, Williams, MacLeish, and Hemingway himself:

Profile: An Anthology Collected in MCMXXXII. Milan: Ferrari, 1932.

Hemingway also owned nine volumes of Pound's prose:

ABC of Economics. [Edition unknown.]

ABC of Reading. Norfolk, Conn.: New Directions, n.d.

Antheil and the Treatise on Harmony. Paris: Three Mountains, 1924.

Gaudier-Brzeska: A Memoir. London: Lane, 1916.

Guide to Kulchur. London: Faber, 1938. [Two copies.]

Lavoro ed usura: Tre saggi. Milan: All'Insegna del Pesce d'Oro, 1954.

Make It New: Essays. [Edition unknown.]

Pavannes and Divagations. Norfolk, Conn.: New Directions, 1958. [Two copies.]

Pavannes and Divisions. [Edition unknown.]

Hemingway also acquired two copies of D. D. Paige's edition of *The Letters of Ezra Pound, 1907-1941*, which was published in 1950 by Harcourt, Brace.

The other 20th Century poet whose career Hemingway followed with considerable attention was T. S. Eliot. Once again, the volumes were acquired over a long period of time, and there are volumes of literary and social criticism as well as poetry. Although Hemingway certainly knew of Eliot's work when he was in Paris in the 1920's, the earliest surviving Eliot volume in the library is a 1929 Faber edition *of Dante.* This volume has a sticker in the back that indicates that it was purchased at Shakespeare and Co. in Paris. Probably, therefore, Hemingway acquired it during his visit to Paris in 1931. His interest in Eliot was still active over twenty years later, when he acquired a copy of *The Complete Poems and Plays.* The following is a complete list of the titles by Eliot in Hemingway's library:

After Strange Gods: A Primer of Modern Heresy. [Edition unknown.]

The Cocktail Party. New York: Harcourt, Brace, 1950.

Collected Poems, 1909-1935. New York: Harcourt, Brace, 1936.

The Complete Poems and Plays. New York: Harcourt, Brace, 1952.

Dante. London: Faber, 1929.

From Poe to Valery. New York: Harcourt, Brace, 1948.

Murder in the Cathedral. [Edition unknown.]

Poems, 1909-1925. London: Faber, 1933.

Selected Essays. [Edition unknown.]

The Use of Poetry and the Use of Criticism: Studies in the Relation of Criticism to Poetry in England. London: Faber, 1933.

There are as many volumes by Archibald MacLeish in Hemingway's library as by Eliot, but in general there is not the same impression of intense interest conveyed by the three collected editions of Eliot's poems. We have no evidence that Hemingway acquired the collected edition of MacLeish's poetry published in 1953. Furthermore, MacLeish and Hemingway knew each other well and some, at least, of the MacLeish volumes were given to Hemingway by MacLeish as gifts. For example, the 1948 edition of *Actfive and Other Poems* is inscribed by MacLeish to Hemingway. The following are the volumes by MacLeish in Hemingway's Library:

Actfive and Other Poems. New York: Random House, 1948.

Air Raid: A Verse Play for Radio. [Edition unknown.]

America Was Promises. [Edition unknown.]

Conquistador. Boston: Houghton Mifflin, 1933.

The Hamlet of A. MacLeish. [Edition unknown.]

New Found Land Fourteen Poems. [Edition unknown.]

Public Speech: Poems. [Edition unknown.]

Songs for Eve. Boston: Houghton Mifflin, 1954.

Streets in the Moon. Boston: Houghton Mifflin, 1926.

The Trojan Horse. Boston: Houghton Mifflin, 1952.

Various other 20th Century poets writing in English are represented by multiple volumes in the library, but in none of these cases does the diversity or chronological range of the volumes indicate a depth of involvement comparable to that demonstrated by the Pound and Eliot holdings. Three poets who do stand out, however, are W. H. Auden, William Butler Yeats, and Edna St. Vincent Millay. The volumes by Auden are:

Another Time: Poems. New Yark: Random House, 1940.
The Collected Poetry of W. H. Auden. New York: Random House, 1945.
Look, Stranger! London: Faber, 1936.
Poems. [Edition unknown.]
(With Christopher Isherwood). *The Ascent of F6: A Tragedy in Two Acts*. London: Faber, 1937.
(With Christopher Isherwood). *The Dog Beneath the Skin; or, Where is Francis?* A Play in Three Acts. London: Faber, 1935.

The volumes by Yeats are:
Autobiographies: Reveries over Childhood and Youth and *The Trembling of the Veil*. [Edition unknown.]
Collected Poems. Definitive edition with the author's final revisions. New York: Macmillan, 1957.
Dramatis Personae, 1896-1902, Estrangement, The Death of Synge,
The Bounty of Sweden. New York: Macmillan, 1936.
Later Poems. New York: Macmillan, 1924.
Poems. [Edition unknown.]

The volumes by Millay are:
Collected Sonnets. New York: Harper, 1941.
Letters. Edited by Allan Ross Macdougall. New York: Harper, 1952.
Poems. [Edition unknown.]
Poems Selected for Young People. New York: Harper, 1929.
Second April. [Edition unknown.]

Hemingway also owned five volumes by William Carlos Williams, but he was clearly more interested in Williams' prose than in his poetry:

> *Autobiography.* New York: Random House, 1951.
> *Life Along the Passaic River.* [Edition unknown.]
> *Selected Poems.* Introduction by Randall Jarrell. New York: New Directions, 1949.
> *A Voyage to Pagany.* [Edition unknown.]
> *White Mule.* [Edition unknown.]

Two additional 20th Century poets writing in English are represented in the library by four volumes. These are Marianne Moore and E. E. Cummings. In the case of Marianne Moore, Hemingway's interest was long-lasting and included the purchase of the collected edition of her poems published in 1951:

> *Collected Poems.* New York: Macmillan, 1951. .
> Marriage. New York: Wheeler, 1923.
> *Predilections.* New York, Vikings, 1955.
> *Selected Poems.* Introduction by T. S. Eliot. New York: Macmillan, 1935.

The volumes by Cummings in the library are:

> *Eimi.* New York: Covici, Friede, 1933.
> *The Enormous Room.* With an introduction by the Author. New York: Modern Library, 1922.
> *Is 5.* New York: Boni & Liveright, 1926.
> *1 x 1.* New York: Bolt, 1944.

When one turns to the 19th Century poets with whom Hemingway was most seriously involved, Charles Baudelaire and Lord Byron, the early publication dates of some of the volumes of their works in Hemingway's possession make it difficult to ascertain when he first read their works. Other information is available, however, which makes it clear that Hemingway was involved with their work over a considerable span of time. It seems likely that he first encountered Baudelaire's works in Paris during the 1920's. It is highly probable that when he lived in Key West in the 1930's he owned a copy of Baudelaire's *Intimate Journals*, translated by Christopher Isherwood, with an introduction by T. S. Eliot. In 1941, a copy of *Les fleurs du mal et complement* was moved from Key West to Cuba. Some time after his return from Europe in 1945, Hemingway acquired a copy of Edwin Morgan's *Flower of Evil: A Life of Charles Baudelaire*, which had been published in 1943 by Sheed & Ward. Finally, in 1948 Hemingway gave Mary Hemingway a copy of Les *fleurs du mal*, with illustrations by Rodin, which he dedicated to her in French. This is a complete list of the volumes by Baudelaire in the library:

> *Les fleurs du mal.* Precedees d'une notice par Theophile Gautier. Paris: C. Levy, 1894.
> *Les fleurs du mal.* Illustrees par Auguste Rodin avec une preface de Camille Mauclair. Paris: The Limited Editions Club, 1940.
> *Lesfleurs du mal et complement.* [Edition unknown.]
> *Lesfleurs du mal.* Stockholm: J an Forlag, 1944.
> *Intimate Journals.* Translated by Christopher Isherwood. Introduction by T. S. Eliot. [Edition unknown.]
> *Morceaux chosis: Poemes et proses.* Introduction et notes par Y. G. Le Dantec. Paris: Gallimard, 1939.

Other French writers seem to have interested Hemingway. A letter to Richard L. Nelson on Sept. 9, 1949, mentions receiving from him copies of Verlaine and Rimbaud. Two volumes by Paul Verlaine are in the library:

> *Oeuvres posthumes. VoL 3: Vers inedits.* Critique et conferences. Appendice. Paris: Messein, 1929.
> *Poemes saturniens.* [Edition unknown, but is among books moved to Cuba in 1941.]

Only one volume by Arthur Rimbaud has survived in the library:

Lettres de la vie litteraire. [Edition unknown.]

In the case of Lord Byron, there can be no doubt that at least by the 1930's Hemingway was fascinated by the Englishman's life—more so, perhaps, than by his poetry. A 1933 Dent edition of Byron's letters was moved from Key West to Cuba in 1941. In addition, that same shipment contained three biographies of Byron: those by Peter Quennell, Harold Nicolson, and Andre Maurois. It is equally clear that this fascination never waned, for in 1957 Hemingway acquired a copy of Leslie Marchand's three-volume life of Byron. The following are the works by Byron in Hemingway's library:

Byron, A Self-portrait: Letters and Diaries, 1798 to 1824, with Hitherto Unpublished Letters. Edited by Peter Quennell. New York: Scribner, 1950.
Child Harold's Pilgrimage. [Edition unknown.]
The Complete Poetical Works. Boston: Houghton Mifflin, 1905.
Don Juan: A Satirical Epic of Modern Life. New York: Heritage, 1943.
His Very Self and Voice: Collected Conversations. Edited by Ernest J. Lovell, Jr. New York: Macmillan, 1954.
The Letters of George Gordon, 6th Lord Byron. Selected by R. G. Howarth with an introduction by Andre Maurois. London: Dent, 1933.
The Life, Letters and Journals of Lord Byron. [Edition unknown.]
Poetical Works. [Edition unknown.]

Seven biographies of Byron are also in the library:

Quennell, Peter. Byron: *The Years of Fame.* New York: Viking, 1935.
Quennell, Peter. *Byron in Italy.* New York: Viking, 1941.

Origo, Iris. *The Last Attachment*: The Story of Byron and Teresa Guiccioli As Told in Their Unpublished Letters and Other Family Papers. New York: Scribner, 1949.

Nicolson, Harold George. Byron: *The Last Journey*. London: Constable, 1934.

Mayne, Ethel Colburn. *Byron*. [Edition unknown.]
Maurois, Andre. *Byron*. 2 vols. [Edition unknown.]

Marchand, Leslie A. *Byron: A Biography*. 3 vols. New York: Knopf, 1957.

Hemingway owned copies of the works of many of the standard English and American poets. The following volumes, for example, are in his library:

The Complete Poetry and Selected Prose of John Donne and The Complete Poetry of William Blake in One Volume. New York: Random House, 1941.

The Poetical Works of John Keats. [Edition unknown.]

Alexander Pope. *Complete Poetical Works*. Boston: Houghton Mifflin, 1903.

The Poetical Works of John Milton. New York: Burt, n.d.

Dante Gabriel Rossetti. *The Poetical Works*. New York: Crowell, n.d.

Percy Bysshe Shelley. *Selected Poetry and Prose*. Edited with an introduction by Carlos Baker. New York: Modern Library, 1951.

William Wordsworth. *The Prelude*; with a Selection from the Shorter Poems. [Edited by Carlos Baker. New York: Rinehart]

Emily Dickinson. *Poems*. Boston: Little, Brown, 1952.

Walt Whitman. *Leaves of Grass*. [Edition unknown.]

Walt Whitman. *Poems and Prose*. [Edition unknown.]

In closing, it is appropriate to mention a work that appears to have had some special significance to Hemingway. This is Shakespeare's Sonnets. In Mary Hemingway's personal library there is an edition of the sonnets, edited by M. R. Ridley and published in London by Dent in 1938. The volume is signed by Hemingway with the note "Re-read

Kenya 1957." Mary Hemingway remarked on several occasions that she often read poetry to Hemingway at night and that The Sonnets was one of the volumes she would read. In her autobiography, *How It Was*, she gives this account of reading to Hemingway when he was ill with hepatitis in the mid 1950's:

> I bought a reading lamp to put behind the chair
> at the foot of his bed and many evenings read aloud
> all sorts of people, from Shakespeare (the sonnets) to
> T. E. Lawrence to Jim Corbett to Anne Morrow Lind-
> bergh to The Oxford Book of English Verse.[37]

In addition to the Dent edition of the sonnets and a number of complete works of Shakespeare that included the sonnets, there are in the library two translations of the sonnets into Italian. This is, of course, only a brief introduction to the interest in poetry listed in our record in the Composite Library, but gathering the titles in even a superficial view reveals a writer devoted to poetic expression as he invented his own prose.

Chapter 3

HEMINGWAY'S DOCTOR:
JOSÉ LUIS HERRERA SOTOLONGO
REMEMBERS ERNEST HEMINGWAY

Dr. José Luis Herrera Sotolongo was Hemingway's close friend and his personal physician for almost twenty years. He met Hemingway while they were both assigned to the Twelfth International Brigade near Madrid in 1937. When the Civil War was over, Herrera was incarcerated by Franco for his activities on behalf of the Loyalists. When exiled to Cuba Herrera resumed medical practice and later became a close associate of Che Guevera and Fidel Castro. Although Herrera was mentioned briefly by Carlos Baker in his biography of Hemingway,[1] Baker never reported Herrera's detailed knowledge of Hemingway's activities in Spain and Cuba. Most important, Herrera's knowledge of Hemingway's relation to the Cuban revolution has never been published in the West.

The most complete record of Hemingway in Cuba was developed over a three-year period by Iuri Paparov, an official of the Russian news agency, *Novisti*, while he was stationed in Cuba. His report on Cuba was published in Russia, but has not been published in the West. After returning to Russia he completed *Kheminguei na Kube* [Hemingway in Cuba], published by the Soviet Writer's Union in 1974.[2] As has been pointed out to me, Dr Herrera presented some confusion of dates and spellings. Since the interviews with him were conducted in Spanish and then his rather patriarchal Spanish was translated into Russian and then finally into English by friends of mine, I am reluctant to adjust place names, dates and campaigns as Dr Herrera reported them.Contemporary readers can make their own adjustments. Paparov's investigations, provide the most comprehensive and, according to Dr. Herrera, the deepest insights into Hemingway's life in Cuba. Unfortunately Paparov's volume has not been translated into English and my extensive inquiries about copyright permissions from the author have not been answered.[3]

The earliest account of Hemingway by Dr. Herrera was recorded privately by Felipe Cunill, a young researcher from the *Instituto de Libres* in Havana, who interviewed Dr.Herrera in Spanish on November 28, 1970. This interview is appended to Paparov's chapter on Dr Herrera and reprinted here.

A second interview with Dr. Herrera was conducted by Laurel Dean Graham early in 1971 while she was associated with the Canadian Embassy in Havana and was conducting research for an article on Hemingway's life in Cuba which was later published in *The Globe Magazine*. The portion of the original article which dealt primarily with Dr. Herrera was omitted from the published version.[4]

The latest source of information on Dr. Herrera was an interview conducted at my request by Mary Cruz, a Cuban biographer/critic of Hemingway, and Dr. Angel Augier, Vice President of the Cuban Union of Artists and Writers in February, 1984.[5] The interviewers were pleased to report that Dr Herrera, then about seventy-one years old, was alert, in good health, and still active as chief of the medical section of the General Staff of the Civil Defense Department in Cuba.[6]

Dr. Herrera first met Hemingway in Spain in 1937. Herrera was Chief of Surgery Services for the Twelfth International Brigade(Cruz) located at *Moratas de Tajufia* while the Brigade was preparing for the "*Jarama*" offensive. The Brigade had suffered many casualties in the battle for Madrid and was regrouping after having received excessive losses at *La Casa de Campo, El Pardo, Las Rosas,* and *Villaneuva del Pardillo* (Cunill) and the brief success at *Brihuega*. Late in December

1936 the chief medical officer of the Brigade, Bernard Heilung, asked Herrera to drive into Madrid and pick up an American newspaper reporter who wanted to spend a few days with the Brigade. Herrera did as requested and found Martha Gellhorn waiting at the *Hotel Floridita*. She had been commissioned by *Collier's* to do an article on the Brigade. Herrera returned her to the Brigade hospital which also functioned as a sort of tourist hotel. Hemingway was also staying at the *Hotel Florida* on assignment for the North American Newspaper Alliance and helping to prepare a documentary film [*The Spanish Earth*] intended to arouse American sympathy for the Spanish people and the Loyalist cause. Hemingway had taken a short trip to *Cetafa*, south of Madrid, and when he returned to Madrid and found Martha gone, he was quite upset. In a few days he caught up with her at the Brigade hospital. From then on he made the headquarters of the Brigade his base of operations. Later he said of the Twelfth Brigade that "this was where [his] heart was" (Dean). Some fusion of romantic and political enthusiasms may have informed this admission.

Hemingway stayed with the Twelfth International Brigade for about a month (january 1937) during the offensive at "Jarama". He used the Brigade as a center of operations, but he was not there during the important battle of *Guadalahara*. He arrived at the last moment and took many pictures, but the battle against the Italians had been won before he arrived. Hemingway rested with the Brigade at the palace of *Aldama* and at a nearby estate where he played football with the troops (Cunill).

On Monday eve, a few days before Hemingway was to leave for America in order to prepare for the release of *The Spanish Earth* and to finish *To Have and Have Not*, the Twelfth Brigade threw a huge party in *El Palacio de la Moraleja*, the estate of a Spanish *marqueses* which had been converted into a base hospital for the Brigade (Dean). It was evidently a lively party, attended by most senior officers and many of the people who were working on the film with Hemingway. Dr. Herrera explained that Hemingway had a little too much to drink and before long became completely *borracho*. Some of the officers carried Hemingway's limp body into the operating room, laid him on the operating table, tied down his arms and legs, donned surgical gowns and masks, and prepared their instruments. Hemingway woke up just as they were feigning their first incision and started to panic. He admitted to Herrera later that he thought he had been captured by the Fascists and that they were about to cut him in half.

Herrera and Hemingway met again during the attack on *Huesca.* In July 1937 Hemingway was with the Brigade, and later that year he joined it for the attack on *Teruel.* Herrera remarked that Hemingway always had a knack for showing up at the most important battles. After *Teruel,* Herrera and Hemingway lost contact with each other for the duration of the Spanish Civil War (Cunill).

For his role in the Loyalist cause Dr. Herrera spent forty-two days in a concentration camp in 1939 and was then sentenced to thirty years in jail. His father was a Cuban with some influence, however, and after Herrera had served two years of his sentence he was exiled to Cuba. He arrived in Cuba on December 6, 1941, and from that time on he was not only Hemingway's personal physician, but one of his closest friends (Dean). Herrera's recollections of his associations with Hemingway remain to date the most authentic account of a twenty-year period almost entirely neglected by Carlos Baker and others.

Dr. Herrera said that "Ernesto" was like a brother to him. "I knew all of his moods. When he was depressed, he wasn't quarrelsome, but he didn't talk much either. He never went out when he was down; he'd drink at home, instead, to cheer himself up." Then he added, "There is a fantasy about Ernesto's drinking habits. He was not a drunk. I had read somewhere that Hemingway had cirrhosis of the liver, but that was not true." There was a time in the late forties, though, when Hemingway's drinking became habitual. Herrera criticized him severely and even sent a letter resigning as his physician, but Hemingway apologized and Herrera remained loyal to him (Dean). Herrera also records a bout of hepatitis that Hemingway suffered in the mid 1950s. Hemingway spent three months in bed, during which Rene Villereal, the house manager, told all visitors that Hemingway was not at home. During this time he was rationed to one ounce of whiskey in the afternoon and one in the evening, and the only persons who were allowed access to him were Dr. Herrera and a few very close friends (Dean).

Dr. Herrera recounted an incident on the Pilar when Hemingway opened his skull down to the bone after falling against one of the large clamps that held the gaffs in place. Roberto Herrera, Jose's brother, saved Hemingway's life by fashioning a tourniquet alongside the left eye to stop the arterial blood from spouting until they could get Hemingway back to *Finca Vigia*. At the *Finca*, Dr. Herrera advised Hemingway that an anesthetic was necessary while he closed the wound, but Hemingway refused. Herrera demanded that he remain absolutely immobile. When a maid assisting Dr. Herrera spilled a bottle of alcohol over Hemingway's bare knees just as Herrera was finishing, Hemingway didn't budge. Dr. Herrera said incredulously, "Why didn't you move, Ernesto?" Hemingway replied, unshaken, "I was waiting for your permission."

Dr. Herrera knew that Hemingway was in deep trouble when he left Cuba for the last time. He had always received regular letters from him when he was abroad, but this time nothing appeared. Although many professors have learned to answer student queries about Hemingway's suicide with vague references to Hotchner's biography[7] (which Dr. Herrera doubts fundamentally) and to the obvious fact that Hemingway was very ill when he committed suicide, Dr. Herrera tells a chilling story of troubled times on board the Pilar:

> [Hemingway] had the obsession to commit sui-
> cide. He always said he was going to commit suicide,
> which he did, and he even [demonstrated how he
> would do it]. "See how I am going to kill myself," and
> he would take the posture in which he killed himself.
> He killed himself with a shotgun, putting the barrel
> in his mouth and shooting with the big toe. He tried
> it many times on several occasions when he had pri-
> vate problems of a depressing nature and he was con-
> templating suicide. (Cunill)

Herrera repeated tales of some difficult times during the late 1940s at Finca Vigia. The account of the period retold by Paparov in "Indian Blood, " a chapter which suggests Hemingway's affinity with the suicidal Indian father in "Indian Camp," reveals that suicide was seldom far from Hemingway's mind. Herrera related to Paparov that after one particularly bitter family squabble (Adriana Ivancich had recently been on the scene) he left Finca Vigia in despair and wrote the following letter to his close friend:

Dear Ernesto:

This night I shared the sleeplessness with you. I was a witness of your anxieties and your troubles. I have analyzed them and understood the nature of your problems. Your sincere confession enabled me to perceive and to feel the whole force of your anxieties. I understand them. It is the nature of man and at the same time it is marvelous to submit yourself to the power of the weakness which will inevitably weaken your sense of judgment and keep it unchained, gradually substituting pain for joy, despair for hope and anxiety in place of tranquility. I understand you Ernesto, and I am capable of evaluating the seriousness of your spiritual state. Your problem has not material substance or basis and can be rectified. Passion can choke it with innumerable weight, and a person is capable of using the ability correctly that has taken place before his very eyes. When he is overcome with great tenderness and he is experiencing serious love, however, you must not forget that the spiritual forces of man are hardened when they are prepared to face similar attacks that are capable of struggling or surviving. You're a man who can glorify the carnal and spiritual emotions, who is capable of exceeding the boundaries of ordinary life to plunge into the world of feelings and spiritual experiences, and you often enter this unreal world created by the means of your exalting fantasy, but this time you are in love not with the subject of your love, but with love itself, with your own feeling of love. You exult love for other people, the love that you are experiencing because there were other men who would have perceived the end of their desires, you seek something beyond that. You must not give in to a free reign of your feelings. Do not substitute the colorful play of the horizon for a pitiful gray luster of disenchantment for you are not certain that your new feeling shall be the last one. Can you be certain that having satisfied your moral and physical passions you shall be able to turn it into the complete happiness that you are seeking? And are you certain of the fact that you are truly in love once again, and that you are not merely a captive of a swiftly passing passion? Your spiritual strength is still very firm and still far from demise, and therefore, you must understand that they must lure you into other horizons. This is not the last word. It is only a tremolo that shall disappear with the sound of a new note.

A genius is the fruit of the spirit. He is eternal. You are endowed with genius and are capable of creating of your own accord your own spiritual life. You are living in a constant spiritual enthusiasm. It is possible that this may be the source of your great problems. You are capable of analyzing that which you are creating, but perhaps you did not reflect duly on the emotions or feelings embracing you at this very moment. Because it seems to you to be boundless and immeasurable, you are afraid of it. It is afraid of you and you as an infant are singing in order to dispel fear and endeavoring to get rid of the spirits that have taken a hold of your soul, in a creative manner causing its body to return to a lethargic sleep with the aid of wine. No, that is not the burden which you should bear. You should not take those pains. You should be struggling with your own self. If your alter ego endows you with feelings, if that is leading you into despair, lead out the yearnings of your soul into a past that is necessary for you. Become a master of them and make use of that which brings you pain for the sake of self-interest. I am aware how difficult it is to realize what I am talking about or that I am capable of understanding the extent to which you are nurtured by life. Everything is accessible to you because now you long for something great. You have achieved more than one victory. You have satisfied your source of income and you have experienced the pleasure of your labors.

It is impossible and somehow this influences your present spiritual state.

If you have attained the material on your own, through a courageous struggle of your own, you should not be discouraged at this time. You are oversaturated and, therefore, you are creating phantoms of illusions. Do not allow your imagination to overwhelm you. Direct its force into positive aspects, and then perhaps you shall be in a position to attain some peace to pacify the turbulent manifestations of your feelings. You must not allow hopelessness and despair to overwhelm you. You have no right to destroy an intellect which was sent only to you because you are making use of it at the moment in order to leave a heritage for mankind, but you must not torment your soul, devouring it by way of experiences on the occasion of a remote passion. You must not permit them to lure you into an abyss. You must struggle courageously against yourself, introducing into your own spirit such feelings which are more compatible with you. Transpose your love into an ideal in order that it should fulfill the summit of your inspiration. Be brave, Ernesto, and then you shall conquer. Think about who you are and what you are really capable of. Think about that which you are still to become. Remember all of your children, who adore you as a father and admire you as a man. Think about the woman who has given you her love and thinks about nothing but your happiness. She shares your happiness and joys, your sorrows. She loves you, adores you with the very same feeling which you have imagined yourself in respect to another one. Yes, Mary is precisely such a woman, and I feel that you are capable of understanding this. Think about your friends who are totally devoted to you and lastly this, think about the future. It may be a future of rainbow radiance and happiness for you. One error, one false step could turn your future into a hostile existence devoid of all hope to love or exist. Think about that Ernesto. Once again, get a hold of all of your feelings. Love Mary, your children. Love life and once again you will be capable of respecting yourself.

Jose Luis
7 July 1950[8]

Three days later there had been two phone calls for Dr. Herrera from Finca Vigia. When Hemingway called the third time, he said to Herrera, "Forgive me, Feo, I am a complete scoundrel. I am a son of a bitch. Indeed I am. Have you shown the wound to anyone? I am waiting for you. Please come. I beg you" (Paparov). Some confusion appears to surround this letter. Herrera indicated to Cunill that he could not find the letter among his papers which were returned to him by Mrs. Hemingway when she left Cuba. Paparov records a Russian translation of the letter without indicating its specific source, but as the Cunill interview indicates, Herrera was greatly impressed with Paparov's researches and clearly cooperated fully with him. At any rate, despite the fact that what appears above is an English translation of a Russian text that was originally written in Spanish, the letter reveals the deep intimacy between the two men and the level of confidence which Hemingway shared with Herrera. At this time, Herrera was a regular visitor at the Hemingways' and even had his own key to the Finca Vigia, a privilege which he shared with no one.

Perhaps one of the most significant aspects of their relationship involved Herrera's observations on Hemingway's attitude toward the Cuban revolution. From the very beginning of the 26th of July

Movement[9] Herrera had kept Hemingway informed on the progress of the revolution. Herrera and Castro had been close friends ever since their university days when they had lived in the same apartment building on the corner of 3rd Avenue and 2nd Street in Vedado. In addition, Herrera's admiration of Che Guevera bordered on idolatry. Long after Guevera's death, Herrera maintained a virtual shrine to his memory in his apartment (Dean). When Herrera became a medical officer in Castro's bureaucracy shortly after the seizure of power in 1959, he was a good source of "true gen" for Hemingway. For example, early in the development of events that led to Batista's overthrow, Herrera informed Hemingway that an apparently mysterious explosion was caused by Castro and his little band of supporters operating out of the Sierra Maestra Mountains in eastern Cuba (Paparov). Moreover, Herrera hinted that some unofficial meetings of members of the anti-Batista movement had taken place at the Finca Vigia (Cruz). Thus there was perhaps some reason why Batista's military police tried to search *Finca Vigia* during August 1958.

Hemingway always kept his distance from Fulgencio Batista, who had seized power in a military coup during March 1952. Shortly after this Batista had tried to court Hemingway by honoring him with the Order of Carlos Manuel de Cespedes,[10] but Hemingway never returned his overtures. On one occasion when the hunting club, *El Sierra,* of which Hemingway was a prominent member, planned to dedicate its new facilities with a ribbon-cutting ceremony by Batista, Hemingway refused to attend. A blunt summary of his attitude toward the dictator was recorded after Batista fled to the Dominican Republic with what Hemingway estimated to be about eight hundred million dollars and fifty suitcases packed with valuables. Hemingway wrote to Gianfranco Ivancich on January 7, 1959, *Sic transit hijo de puta"* [So passes the son of a whore].[11]

His unfriendly attitude toward Batista suggests that Hemingway had more than passing interest in Castro's revolution. Certainly it reveals that the Cuban expatriot Edmundo Desnoes' assessment of Hemingway's feelings toward Cuba was less than accurate. In *Inconsolable Memories* Desnoes portrayed Hemingway's attitude to Cuba as that of a decadent bourgeois:

> While [the guide at *Finca Vigia*, after Hemingway's death] went into details of Papa's boring house habits, I stood staring at a bald mangy spot on the tiger's head and I thought that Cuba never meant a fucking thing to Hemingway. Boots to hunt in Africa, American furniture, Spanish photographs, books and magazines in English, bullfight posters. Nowhere in the whole house was there anything Cuban, not even an Afro-Cuban witchcraft conversation piece or a painting. Nothing. Cuba, for Hemingway, was just a place where he could take refuge, live quietly with his wife, receive his friends, write in English, fish in the Gulf Stream. Cubans, we meant very little to him.[12]

In light of Herrera's evidence, Desnoes' criticism appears to be harsh, to say the least. Rene Villereal, the Finca Vigia house manager, reported to Paparov (before he moved to New Jersey) that Hemingway encouraged the local rebels in San Francisco de Paula. Recently, Herrera reported that, until he died, Hemingway supported both the Spanish Communist Party and the Communist Party in Guanabacoa, the capital of the municipio [township] in which San Francisco de Paula is located (Cruz).

Herrera's views on Hemingway as a supporter of Castro were reinforced by another old friend from the Spanish Civil War, Herbert Matthews. Matthews had been the first reporter to file a story on Castro and his guerrillas in the Sierra Maestra Mountains in February 1957, and when he returned to Cuba in 1960 for a look at Castro's revolution which was then secure, he visited Hemingway after filing his report. In his diary for March 13, 1960, he entered:

> Ernest Hemingway is still the great hero of the Cuban people. He is staying at his home and working as a deliberate gesture to show his sympathy and support for the Castro revolution. He knows Cuba and the Cuban people as well as any American citizen. I was glad to find that his ideas on Fidel Castro and the Cuban Revolution are the same as mine.[13]

Buried on page nine of the New York Times for 6 November 1959 was the laconic report, "Mr. Hemingway told newsmen he had every sympathy with Prime Minister Fidel Castro's regime." What Matthews and Hemingway agreed upon was that Fidel Castro was successful primarily because he had eliminated the old guard and had effectively destroyed the old system. Even if Castro failed, they agreed, there was no way that Cuba could return to the old system. Hemingway's views on Dr. Castro and the revolution were obviously not comfortable or popular during the cold war antagonism of 1959.

Hemingway was not so quiet, perhaps, about his admiration for Fidel as the American press pretended. Late in February 1958 he was invited to an opening of an art show by the Cuban artist, Maria Pepe La Mot. Hemingway admired his charcoal drawings, especially the landscapes of Mexico and Spain. After almost everyone had left, someone thrust a morning paper into his hand. The headline read: "Victory in Rio del Buddos. The army of the Barbudos has been liquidated." Hemingway yelled, "That's a pack of lies. They can't kill Castro. The patriots will nevertheless be victorious." Everyone near him scattered. Batista's spies were assumed to be everywhere. "Fiction, lies, Batista thinks he can conquer them through victories on paper," Hemingway continued. "Just let him wait. All this is a pack of lies."[14]

The sinister incident which set Hemingway squarely against the Batista regime occurred about August 22, 1957, at *Finca Vigia*.[15] Herrera insisted that this confrontation was the key personal event that forced Hemingway to reflect seriously on the political climate in Cuba.[16] Late one evening when everyone was asleep, Hemingway was disturbed by rifle butts banging against the front door of the Finca Vigia. As he opened the door, he slowly realized what was the matter. Outside his door he saw five armed men, commanded by a sergeant, who demanded to know whether the master of the Finca had seen two peasants whom they wanted to question. Were they hiding in the house? Herrera reported that Hemingway chose his words carefully so as not to arouse the suspicion of the agitated, armed, and intoxicated soldiers. Yet while he was explaining to them that there was no stranger in the house, a young, strong, hunting dog, "Machacos," ran out of the living room and jumped, barking at the soldiers. The sergeant aimed his Thompson at the dog, and the bullets went right through him. Herrera said that Hemingway had to exercise incredible restraint and will power or he would have suffered the same fate as "Machacos." The soldiers capped the incident with much swearing. In the morning Hemingway buried the dog next to the swimming pool. He placed a marker on the spot and fired a farewell shot.[17] Herrera felt that from this moment Hemingway became seriously concerned about the situation in Cuba, and his work was sorely disrupted. Mary advised him to fly to New York, but when he got there he felt even worse. When he returned to *Finca Vigia* he began to live an even more secluded life—he seldom frequented La Floridita and he almost never went to sea (Cunill).

As the Cuban Revolution was approaching its crisis in late 1958, Hemingway was recuperating at his summer home in Ketchum, Idaho. During the second half of December, Hemingway was feeling much better, and Herrera records that since the Hemingways resumed sending Christmas cards, he could assume that Hemingway was feeling better. Hemingway was apparently listening closely to the radio for news of the Castro revolution. Shortly after Batista fled Cuba, Hemingway was on the phone to Herrera: "The Revolution must be saved. Do all you can for it!" (Cruz).

During the same call, he gave instructions to Rene Villereal who had been left in charge of *Finca Vigia*. Hemingway congratulated Rene and all Cubans on the victory. Rene even reported that Hemingway was very cheerful and laughed (Paparov, 405). When Hemingway asked how things were at *Finca Vigia*, Rene replied, "OK," but then had to admit that the local militia detachment associated with the revolution had come to the *Finca* looking for arms. "Give them everything they want to take," Hemingway quickly replied. "Give them all the ammunition. More than that, if they need it, fill the tank [of the pickup truck] and let Hondu [the mechanic] do whatever he's told to do. Should they need the house, for after all it occupies a strategic position, allow them to use it as well" (Paparov). He also instructed Rene, "in an emergency," to loan the station wagon to "responsible local revolutionaries."[18] Hemingway was also pleased to learn that the sergeant who shot "Machacos" had been strung up on a lamppost in San Francisco de Paula because of his loyalty to Batista.

Rene reported Hemingway's enthusiasm for the impending attack on Havana to Ismail, the local commander, and soon the militia came for the pickup truck and the guns. Rene handed over ten rifles and shotguns, one revolver, and all the cartridges. Rene reported to Hemingway that every thing was returned a few days later without a shot having been fired from them (Paparov).

Hemingway was apparently very pleased with how the whole affair was progressing, but when he phoned the Finca Vigia again after the funeral of Colonel Williams on February 18, 1959, he was desperate and crying over the telephone. Rene cheered him up with the news that Herrera had been appointed counselor to the medical division of the rebel army and that another good friend of Hemingway's, High Boffio, had been appointed a member of the provisional government. Hemingway was so pleased with this news about the involvement of his friends in the revolution that he promised to return soon so that he could see this all with his own eyes. Within a month, the Hemingways returned to Cuba.

Castro and Hemingway did not meet until May 16, 1960. At that time they chatted for about half an hour before Hemingway presented Castro with a trophy for winning the annual Hemingway marlin contest. This was well after the widely reported incident which occurred as Hemingway was returning to Cuba from New York. He was greeted by a crowd at the Havana airport and asked by a reporter what he thought of the revolution. Hemingway deplored the American attitude, especially toward Castro, and said that he considered himself a true Cuban and didn't want to be known as a "Yankee." To prove it he leaned over and kissed the Cuban flag. All of the reporters and photographers were caught by surprise and insisted that Hemingway repeat the gesture. "1 said I was a Cuban," he replied, "not an actor."[19]

During July 1959 Castro was being questioned on a television program called, "This is Your [Cuba's] Life." He was asked about the many executions which had been rumored by the press. By way of answer, Castro quoted from an article in a South American newspaper in which Hemingway had been interviewed by Emmett Watson:

> Rebellion against Batista is the first revolution in
> Cuba which should be regarded as a genuine revolu-

tion. Great things can be expected from Castro . . . .
I believe in the objectives of the Cuban revolution.
Cuba had former changes in government, but these
were mere changes of the watchdogs of the sentry. The
first task of the newcomers was always to plunder the
people. Some of those who were close to Batista were
honest people, but the majority were thieves, sadists,
and executioners. And they tortured people, sometimes so ferociously that there was nothing left to do
but finish off the victims. The executions introduced
by Castro are indispensable. If his government does
not shoot those people they will in any case be done
away with by those who seek revenge. As a result an
epidemic of vendettas will take place in the cities and
villages. What will happen to these people if they had
been given amnesty? The people will know who the
wrong-doers are sooner or later and demand retribu-
tion. Castro's movement has been successful because
it has promised to punish those who are responsible
for the mis-deeds. I am in favor of Castro's revolution
because it has the support of the people. I believe in
its cause.

Although Cuban sources and Paparov attest to the existence of
this statement, its authenticity remains in doubt.[20]

A more probable and verifiable indication of Hemingway's
concern for Cuba's welfare occurred during September 1960 when
Castro was scheduled to appear before the General Assembly of the
United Nations in New York. Hemingway was evidently concerned
that the American press would be unduly hostile to Castro. He tried
to get in touch with Castro, and Herrera made a special effort so
that the two of them could meet before Castro spoke to the General
Assembly on September 26, 1960. Hemingway told Herrera, "You
must let [Castro] know that he must know a few things about politics,
about politicians and the idiosyncrasies of the American people. I'll
be able to fill him in on that. His visit there must be triumphant."
Castro was unable to keep their appointment, but sent Vasquez-
Candela, a high-ranking newspaperman with *Revoluccion,* to visit

Hemingway. The roads were dangerous at night at the time, and late one night, shortly before Castro was to depart for New York, Herrera took Vasquez-Candela to Finca Vigia in his car.

Hemingway met them with a pistol. Vasquez-Candela recounted their meeting about three years later:

> I went to San Francisco without being quite sure that Hemingway would consider us directly important. ... I expected to see a proud man whose name had become immortal in world literature, who could not care less about me or anything else, but as soon as I entered the house I felt that the owner was kind, responsive, and friendly in his simplicity and that his only concern was to do everything possible that things would turn out well.

Vasquez-Candela went on to record the meeting in considerable detail. Herrera, Hemingway, and Vasquez-Candela sat in the soft, comfortable chairs in the living room. Mary entered and left. Music played quietly in the background—Beethoven, Bach, Ravel—creating a relaxed and comfortable atmosphere. They drank Italian wine, ate nuts, and spoke about the important meeting to come. Hemingway was most concerned about how the press was tied to the monopolies and would give Castro a difficult time. On the way to the car, Hemingway asked Vasquez-Candela to convey to his comrades how much he supported them.[21]

The complete history of Hemingway's life in Cuba and his enthusiasm for the political developments of the 1950s and 1960s has not yet been written. Statements by Herrera and Paparov must be examined in light of independent and objective evidence. It would be a disservice to Hemingway, however, to ignore this long and significant time of his life when he not only won the Nobel Prize, but achieved world-wide stature and made so many close Cuban friends. Considerable research, especially in the context of his fascination for the American Civil War[22] and his obvious interest in the Spanish Civil War remains to be done. Carlos Baker sums up Hemingway's enthusiasm for Cuba and Dr. Castro with the indifferent suggestion that "The Hemingways did their best to stay clear of Cuban politics."[23] In addition, Baker dismissed Herbert Matthews, Anastas Mikoyan[24] and Castro's revolution in three sentences. 1f as Paparov reports, Hemingway told Mikoyan that, as a result of the revolution Cuba has its first honest government[25] then there is perhaps a great deal of biographical work on Hemingway's life in Cuba to be done—especially by those American critics who one hopes may soon be independent of a large segment of the press and a government dedicated to the destruction of Dr. Castro and his determination to provide the Cuban people with "decent food, education and medical care."[26] The record of Hemingway's life in Cuba is becoming more difficult to research every day. As this writer can testify, Hemingway's library is rapidly deteriorating in the Cuban climate, and those who knew Hemingway personally are quickly disappearing because of age. Attitudes and incidents provided by Norberto Fuentes only complicate what is at best a difficult task. If an accurate picture of Hemingway's life in Cuba and an accurate assessment of his attitude toward the new regime are ever to be preserved, the task must begin at once. Dr. Herrera was only the first of a long list of Cubans who can help us to complete Hemingway's biography from 1938 to 1961.

AN INTERVIEW WITH JOSE LUIS HERRERA SOTOLONGO

This interview was conducted on November 28, 1970, by Filipe Cunill, a researcher from the Instituto de Libres in Havana, Cuba, who was directed to obtain biographical information on Ernest Hemingway. In his search for information beyond the obvious he sought out Dr. Herrera and interviewed him. The interview presented here was obtained from a former director of the Museo Finca Vigia, Raphael Aballi, who supplied it to a researcher associated with the Canadian Embassy. I am indebted to Laurel Dean Graham for granting permission for me to reproduce the interview. The interview was translated by my former colleague, Professor Emeritus Earl Hampel. I am greatly in his debt for the generosity with which he devoted so much time to Dr. Herrera's rather patrician diction and style.

Cunill: When did you first meet Hemingway?

Herrera: I had had the first contacts with him in Spain during the War. We formed our friendship in the Twelfth International Brigade. That was the Brigade I belonged to and where he spent the greatest amount of time. Now when I came to Cuba, I knew that he was living here. I visited him first in 1942. It may be said that Ernest lived practically half his life in Cuba, since he lived here without interruption from 1939 on. Although he made several trips to Africa, he seldom traveled to the United States. It may be said that his life always developed here. Now, Ernest's life was spent very unobtrusively, the majority of the time, because even though he had great prestige as a literary person, and so on, here in Cuba he had not yet reached the fame that he did later. Because of his nature, the routine of his life, he began to get deeper inside of the Cubans, especially with the fishermen because he kept his boat for many seasons in Cojimar. He moved it when he joined the International Sailing Club. Initially he kept it at Cojimar and at that time formed a deep friendship with the fishermen. This gradually gave him a personality here inside Cuba.

Afterwards he took part in the fishing contests. He was frequently present at the "Club of Hill Hunters." He established a nucleus of friends and that gradually increased. In any event, he developed in Cuba a series of problems as a result of the success of his books and his films and gradually the reputation is created that he is odd. There is always a bit of popular imagination at work when there is a character who rises above the norm or about whom they tell a series of legends that are not real. After all there is something here too of a legend with regard to Hemingway. So far as his life here is concerned, it is a very simple life, relatively slight relations because he spends a further part of his time locked up in his estate without having contact with anybody. He was no friend of ostentation nor did he like to receive many people. He used to receive only those who were his friends and that's all.

His life in Cuba reached a high point just before he received the Nobel Prize. When the Nobel Prize arrived he had already acquired a personality which had been created through that contact with the Cuban people, but then the Nobel Prize raised him above it. Official attention then began, and he almost always renounced it. The government allowed many sinecures in the official order of things; it was a swamp in that connection. One of the few things he accepted here was that famous medal of St. Christopher of Habana which they used to give to taxi drivers. Some said they had treated him like a chauffeur on that occasion. No! They had conceded him a medal that was for taxi drivers, not a medal of Havana, and he had accepted that medal. It is not a question of him being vain or proud or anything like that, but he didn't like those things.

During the second world war he had been lending his services to Cuba. He had the responsibility of a series of jobs which were done with the American sub-hunters, and he was a fundamental link between the American naval forces and the government itself. At that period he gained much respect from the government. He was also a friend of President Roosevelt. Later he went to England and took part in the invasion of the European continent. He took part at Normandy. He carried out a series of actions beyond those of war correspondent, which was his official job, as a fighting man. He was linked to fighting units which went ahead of the American army, and when he came back here they granted him a decoration of the United States.

It was one of those stars. I don't know which one. On that occasion it was highly commented on in the local press that he had gone to receive it in the American embassy dressed in a native light blouse. The local press even said that he went in a dirty blouse, but that is not true. He sweated a lot because of his corpulence. I remember the detail because when he reached the Embassy he was carrying a blouse in the car without having put it on, and in the car he changed blouses because during his trip he had sweated from being in the car. The press insisted that he went in a dirty blouse. He was not a proud or vain man, nor did he ever make any great show either of his skill in sports or of his literary or personal viewpoints. After all, he was not a man who worried much about those things.

He had moments of action in relation to Cuba's problem, but he, of course, always acted in the sense of leaning towards the side of democracy, since during the period of tyranny he had his problems out there on his estate. They even tried to search his farm, but he did not allow it. They even killed his dog—the dog that is buried there, Machacos [Blackie]. Those rural soldiers from Santa Maria de Rosario killed it, and when they condemned one of them to thirty years, the public came up and made an uproar. In Santa Maria del Rosario they came out with a petition asking for him to be shot at the beginning of the revolution, and yet they didn't shoot him. He was the head of all the rural policemen that existed there. It was one day that we were present because we used to go to gatherings there on certain days. We didn't gather politically. We might talk. We might comment on what was the news of the day everywhere. I used to go regularly every Wednesday. One day when we went there was a going and coming of cars during the night. I left about twelve o'clock at night or thereabouts. They thought that the meeting was for some conspiring and there was no conspiring or anything. We used to hear the broadcast from the *Sierra Maestra*, and everybody around here listened.

The problems of his last period in Cuba in relation to the Cuban revolution are indeed very interesting. This has not often been appraised, but he was sincerely with the Cuban revolution. He felt great sympathy even for the person of Fidel and the way he focused on problems. They had never been friends, and Fidel had always been an admirer of Hemingway, not just during this time but during all of the time Fidel was in power in Cuba. They came together to fish during the Derby, and I remember, back in 1949, Fidel displayed much interest in getting out to Hemingway's house because he wanted to talk to him and to know him. We never managed to give solid form to that visit. Fidel used to say, "Listen, I wish that you would take me there. I want to know him. I'd be interested in talking to him." Several times I said to Ernest, "I'm going to come with a friend, a chum who wants to know you." But all those activities when he was deeply involved in university politics prevented us from hitting upon a date to go. Later they fished together for the Hemingway trophy.

It was a very strange thing. Possibly one of the most important voices in the world defending the Cuban revolution from the very first moments was Hemingway's voice. And that is not very well-known because on the first of January he made an infrequent trip to Sun Valley for the skiing season. The triumph of the revolution finds him in Sun Valley. In those days they were waging a campaign against the Cuban revolution in the United States in spite of the fact that there was not yet the slightest friction between the United States and Cuba. After that came Fidel's first voyage to the U. S., and there was a vigorous campaign against him, especially in the press, because of some of the trials and shootings that had taken place. Hemingway had to raise his voice in the U. S. against that campaign. It is a little-known fact that the Americans silenced him. He wrote a front-page article for a local newspaper in which he made certain declarations saying that all that propaganda about a blood bath was false and that from what he had known about the trial of the revolutionaries in Cuba he could assure that the number of shootings that had taken place in Cuba didn't even come close to the number of assassinations that had occurred here.

He not only said that in the press, but he recorded it. The recording was turned over to the local broadcasting station, but when the news hit the syndicates, through the newspaper channels, it was suppressed, and no paper in the U. S. reproduced the article. A few days later he returned to Cuba and brought the article with him and sent it to Fidel. I don't remember the name of the Sun Valley newspaper. On one of Fidel's first appearances on television he displayed the newspaper and made some comments on it. He was always present in the Cuban revolution. He would even have died in Cuba if the circumstances of his death had not been so precipitated.

Cunill: What about his suicide?

Herrera: He had the obsession to commit suicide. He always said he was going to commit suicide, which he did, and he even tried [demonstrated] it. "See how I am going to kill myself," and he would take the posture in which he killed himself. He killed himself with a shotgun, putting the barrel in his mouth and shooting with the big toe. He tried [demonstrated] it many times on several occasions when he had private problems of a depressing nature and he was contemplating suicide.

Cunill: What about the Hotchner book and his running down of Hemingway?

Herrera: I have not read it, nor have I read his brother's book. I have kept away from those things. For me, I want to keep the figure of Ernest as I know him and not as they try to paint him now. Especially people who didn't know him. I wouldn't authorize his brother to write a book. That was a pretty nasty act. All he did was exploit the personality of his brother to get money, and I think that between brothers that is not the finest thing. Ernest's brother did not have ....

Cunill: There was a difference of sixteen years between their ages and so the two of them did not coincide much. The biography is more interesting insofar as it covers the ambience in which Hemingway developed in his first years. As for the rest he is using the same sources that others have used.

Herrera: Yes, of course.

Cunill: You never saw Hotchner here in Cuba with Hemingway?

Herrera: I don't remember him, really. I know that he came here, but I don't remember him. I had a fair number of relations with all his friends, and I don't remember him now nor whether he was here. It is possible that he had some relations with him. He had relations with a good many people, but those intimate relations that many today try to appropriate are uncertain. I knew Ernest, and there was no man who could easily become intimate with him. He had a rather difficult nature, and I know the way he was. He accepted only those real friends that he had. There was one of his friends who was an old man from the western part of the States, called a Colonel. He was a real, true friend, but the others only presumed to say that they were his friends. One with whom he had a pretty deep friendship and with whom he had a close relationship was John Dos Passos. Gary Cooper used to come, and indeed he had free entry into the house. He had three or four friends who could always come. Others he received more or less at a distance. He was very difficult. He might invite them one day to lunch. He was courteous. He was an educated man and knew how to keep the formalities, but when he was not interested in a person, he would say no. It is for that reason that I say it is strange that now so many intimates should come forward and try to give the impression that they have been having all their lives with him. I know this is uncertain and that there is a great deal of that.

Here in Cuba, for example, a very profound study of Hemingway has been made by a Russian, Yuri Paparov, director of *Novisti*. This is perhaps the best biographical study that can come out. Yuri has spent three years carefully researching Ernest's life. I don't think that there can be any biographer who has worked so intensely as that man has worked, because he has sought all the roads that there were in order to acquire even minute pieces of information about Hemingway's life. Each time that he discovered a conversation with somebody whom Ernest had seen only once, he would go and see that person. He spent three years working like a real detective. He's published a sketch. He sent me an advanced copy of the book which I have in my possession, although I do not have it at home at this moment because a friend has offered to translate it.

I received two copies of a Soviet literary magazine, *Flag*, in which there are two excerpts from the book. Yuri spent hours here that add up to days and months. The two of us sat here talking, and he picked my brain every night. He used to come and spend three or four hours here with questionnaires which he brought all made up in order to research and get deep into the subject. Maybe that will be one of the best biographical works which will be done about him, and he never knew Ernest .... He is a Russian who speaks Spanish very well. You probably will have known him. He's been here as the director of *Novisti* for three years. He had previously been in Argentine and Mexico. He spoke Spanish perfectly.

Cunhill: Did he go to the U. S.?

Herrera: Who? Yuri? No. He was the director of *Novisti* in Argentina, and from there he went to Mexico. From Mexico he went to Cuba and then returned to the Soviet Union. He sent me the magazines from the Soviet Union about two months ago. It is interesting because he has gone very deeply into Ernest's life. I don't know how the book will turn out because sometimes I've seen famous writers take many notes for a book and then out comes a calamity. I knew a German writer, Gustav Regler, who was fighting in the Spanish war as a political commissary, and every night he would fill several notebooks with small script about events of the day. He kept a diary which possibly had no equal as a war diary, and yet when the book came out on the war in Spain it was a real disaster. It's called *The Great Crusade*. It has no literary value, and the fact that Ernest wrote a prologue for him to facilitate the book was all right because they were good friends.

Cunill: What about Hemingway in the International Brigade?

Herrera: Yes, he was not there as a fighting man. He was there as a correspondent. I knew him as follows: we were there together after the operations on the Madrid front terminated. The Twelfth Brigade brought us together in an area to the west of Madrid with the intention of regrouping because we had suffered many casualties. We had been in successive battles from November in the *La Casa de Campo, El Pardo, Las Rosas, Villanueva del Pardillo*, a whole series of successive battles, and it was the Twelfth International Brigade that almost single-handedly carried the weight in all these battles. At this time during the last days of December we were making a short offensive on *Brihuega*. We took *Brihuega*. We left there the forces of the Fourth Battalion and we'd come back to Madrid, but in the last battle that we had for Madrid, *Las Rosas*, we suffered many casualties. The Brigade remained in quite deplorable conditions with regard to casualties and the personnel and equipment were worn out, and then they gave us a reinforcement in the east of Madrid, a town called *Moratas de Tajuna*. We had one of the battalions, the other was in *Perales*, and we were spread out. Since a Brigade is never going to concentrate in a single place to rest, we distributed it, and there we were when the head of health of the Brigade comes, a German called Bernard Heilung, and one afternoon he said to me, "You're the best-dressed officer. Go to Madrid and pick up an American newspaper man who wants to come and spend a couple of days with us and do a story. In the Hotel Florida, you will find my wife, Matilde, waiting fo you." There, in fact was the wife of this doctor, Bernard Heilung, with an American woman who turned out to be Martha Gellhorn, who was later Ernest's wife. We got into the jeep and we took off, and then we settled her in the hospital of the Twelfth Brigade, which also served as a sort of tourist hotel. Ernest at that time was in love with her. He had gone to the front, south of Madrid, in the area around *Getafa*, and when he returned to the hotel, Martha was not there. He followed her to the Twelfth Brigade and seemed to like it there. From that time on the Twelfth brigade was his constant point of meeting.

The greater part of the time he spent living with us, and from there he went out and did his job. He always had a sincere attitude of helpfulness toward the Spanish Republic, even though he had had many arguments about that. I can assure you that he was very enthusiastic and convinced about the rationale of the Spanish people, although there are those who have tried to distract somewhat from his person, basically because of the things that he wrote in *For Whom the Bell Tolls*.

This book is a very easy and a very difficult book. I've argued with him. We've talked profoundly at times about the book, Ernest and I, and we came to the conclusion that in fact the book has not been interpreted correctly by all those who read it. Some interpreted it as an adventure. Others consider it a book of war action, and others consider it as an attack on different aspects of Spanish politics. None of them is right. The book has one point of deep meaning. It is not precisely an episode. It is the impact of the Spanish war on Ernest. He interprets it perhaps a bit novelistically, coming close to a newspaper story at some times, but in reality it pours out the intimate feeling that he has for the Spanish people.

When he reached the Twelfth Brigade, Martha had been there for several days, and he stayed and he was our guest for a long time. He visited us first during early January 1937, when we were at *Moratas de Tajufia*. After that he spent almost a month with us during the entire offensive of the *Jarama*.

Then there was a lapse when he went off to other fronts while we were carrying out the operation of *Cuadalahara* against the Italians. He was not there. He arrived at the last moment. When he saw that it was an attack of great importance, he went there immediately and arrived precisely when we had turned a palace into a hospital. By the time he arrived we had already left, and he took several pictures which he has on his estate. He rested with the Twelfth Brigade in the palace of *Aldama* .... He rested with us all the time in the estate at *Moralaja*. We had football games there and later he left. We met again when he returned from Aragon. We were carrying out the operation on

Huesca, where General Lucas was killed, and we established contact when we returned again from Madrid. This would be about July 1937, when the U. S. attacked the anti-fascist intellectuals who went there. That was the convention where Marinello, Nicolas Guillen, and some others attended. We were together again on that occasion when Gustav Regler was wounded. He had gone with General Lucas, and an artillery shell struck the mobile unit and Lucas died, with his chauffeur, and Gustav Regler remained in very serious condition. Since it was a head wound, he remained out of action for a long time. I think he is well now. He was a paralytic for some time.

Ernest joined the Twelfth Brigade sometime after it had been transformed into a division and began the offensive on *Teruel*. During the taking of *Teruel*, Ernest landed with us. He always involved in the most important operations. We got together again, but a few days later he was transferred to the front and then we lost contact.

We established contact again when I came out here. I went to see him, and from the moment I arrived here we did not lose a common bond since I frequently spent weekends in his house and I went regularly every day. I used to go every Wednesday, every month of the year, so that we would not lose contact. In the beginning I used to go every ten or twelve days, and then we planned it this way and every Wednesday, come what may, I had to go there. During the times when my family was in the U. S. I used to finish my work on Friday, and I spent Friday night and all day Saturday and all day Sunday. Monday morning I used to come into Havana again. It was a life of real intimacy because the friendships made in war are pretty deep ones, and at no moment did we have any arguments. We had differences about various things, more or less violent sometimes, but they were never sufficient to weaken our friendship.

Cunill: Hemingway had a rather difficult nature in the sense that he had problems with some of his very close friends. Perhaps because of that very affection that he professed to them. He had a problem also with John Dos Passes.

Herrera: Okay. The problems that he had with me were very private ones. There was a season when he did not keep the proper composure. It was too much drink. I was always watching somewhat his drinking because that had become legendary. He drank more than is generally known in that he drank directly from the bottle. For those of us who were accustomed to the life of the drinking man in Spain or France where men drink, he was not an extraordinary drinker. Any person in those countries used to drink more than he did. Here it attracted more attention because a legend about his drinking grew up. There was a time when he began to drink so that he was not able to write. It was then that I said to him, "If you keep on drinking this way you're not going to be able to write your name." It was the season when he became an alcoholic. It was ominous for us because I don't like people who drink and I told him so: "Chico, you have transformed yourself into a habitual drunkard and I repudiate that kind of person. If you are an habitual drunkard I can do without your friendship of ours if you don't change yourself. I have tried so far as I could to get you to stop it and if I don't succeed there will be nothing for us to do but to go our separate ways."

Cunill: That was about the end of the forties?

Herrera: That was during the forties. The war ended in forty-five. I suppose in about forty-eight or thereabouts we really broke off one day. That was when the rupture occurred. It was one night when there was a family problem between Mary and him. When I returned home, I wrote him a letter and I sent it to him the next day with my brother, and then he called me on the phone and asked me to come and see him. I went to see him and he told me that in fact I was right and that he felt very sorry and since I was so offended he was going to rectify it. I should try to help him and we should not break off. So the affair was settled.

Many times afterwards we spoke of that, and I don't know where the letter is. All my letters to him appeared, but not that one because Mary handed me everything that she had of mine before she left. She gave me a file that he had with my letters and she told me that I should keep them. But that letter I have not found. Ernest was a man who didn't throw away a piece of paper. I've seen letters written to him. Like myself he liked to collect stamps. He used to tell me to tear off the stamps from those letters, but I wouldn't tear them off. I knew how he was. He liked to have the letters as he had received them, and years would go by when the bed was always filled with letters. He never slept in that bed. He knew things were there, but no one else knew it. He had his order within disorder. There came a time when his files were so great that my brother, the one who was in the museum when he didn't have a job, was asked by Ernest to stay with him as a secretary so that he could organize all his files, all his correspondence, all his letters. Everything was filed. What a pile of papers there was in that house.

Cunill: Where are those papers?

Herrera: I don't know where all that ended up. There were even problems with the Nobel Prize medal. It was lost for a long time, and I was one of those who had the greatest influence on Hemingway to get the medal to appear. He used to say, "Now let's leave it; it doesn't mean anything. It can't be lost." It turned up during the revolution, according to what they told me. I've been assured that it was in security. That was the fate that he gave it, but that fate was not the real fate because there have been false interpretations about that too. He didn't give the medal to the Virgin or anything like that. He gave it to the people of Cuba, thinking that at that period those who were governing Cuba were thieves and the only place that it might be secure was in the *Santuario del Cobro*. It was the safest place it could be and that was why he didn't worry about it being lost for almost two years.

Cunill: Hemingway was a religious man?

Herrera: No, he was not religious. He had no religion. He had no religious sentiment. In his daily language he was a blasphemer, but he did have some protection from the Jesuits. That came from his family ancestors. He was protected by the Jesuits in the sense that he could count on their help at a given moment or hide in their convents or make use of them. They even sent him a review from the States, but he was not religious. He had no religion. He was completely materialistic in that sense. He had superstitions, but no religion. He was superstitious about a number of things. Although he had contact with a priest, a very great friendship, it was with a priest who had very special conditions. He was my friend too, and although I did not like those friendships with exiled Spaniards, he had very great merit. He was a liberal man in addition to being a priest. He was a man who could live alongside of us if we had not been able to live alongside of him. His religious feelings were that of a priest, but socially he didn't consider himself to be a priest, but was anticlerical. He used to say that, but there were many facts that proved the very correct position of that man.

[Here ends the interview, although Aballi's notes indicate that there were *additional* pages in which Herrera talked about himself and the role of the Cubans in the Spanish Civil War.]

Chapter 4

INVENTION FROM KNOWLEDGE: THE HEMINGWAY-COWLEY CORRESPONDENCE

MALCOLM Cowley once tried to write a full-length biography of Ernest Hemingway, and it took the combined fury of both Hemingway and his wife to dissuade him. Perhaps he knew too much. His poetic memorial suggests that he was closer to "that other Hemingway" than most critics and readers of Hemingway.

ERNEST

Safe is the man with blunderbus
who stalks the hippopotamus
on Niger's bank or scours the veldt
to rape the lion of his pelt;

but deep in peril he who sits
at home to rack his lonely wits
and there do battle, grim and blind,
against the jackals of the mind.[1]

Hemingway as the man who battled against "the jackals of the mind" seldom appears in the biographical record to date, and

Cowley's failure to produce an extended biography of Hemingway is a great loss. Hemingway, writing from Italy in 1951, admitted to Cowley, "I think you know more about my writing than anybody probably except possibly me."[2] Their correspondence and friendship lasted many years and survived many arguments.[3] The exchange of seventy-one letters began with two random letters in 1937 and 1940, gathered momentum in September 1947, after Cowley had edited *The Portable Hemingway*,[4] continued through the period when Cowley was commissioned to write a major article on Hemingway for *Life* magazine,[5] and progressed through the publication of *Across the River and into the Trees* (1950) until it ended shortly after the publication of *The Old Man and the Sea* (1952).

The period during which this correspondence took place started with the Spanish Civil War and centered largely on the post-World War II era. They discussed the surge of postwar fiction, the Korean War, and the McCarthy menace. The correspondence ranged far and wide over the landscape of these events and included comments on John Horne Burns, John Dos Passos, James Jones, Norman Mailer, Maxwell Perkins, J. D. Salinger, Charles Scribner, and Thomas Wolfe, among others. They discussed the relation of the new "war poets" to their experience and the old problems about how critics misunderstood writers and how editors mismanaged authors. In addition, they drew each other out on subjects as diverse as Dante and copyright laws, gardening and Hiirtgenwald, the Rambouillet affair and Robert Lowell's paranoia.[6]

Hemingway was undoubtedly lonely for literary conversation in Cuba, and his letters to Cowley frequently took the place of informal conversations about literature and literary personalities. Beneath all of the exchanges runs a mutual concern for the literary scene that Hemingway and Cowley explored with depth and reflection. Since Hemingway considered himself a "worldclass" writer, he frequently reflected on his writing in the context of other important writers and their works. He was willing to discuss the process by which his fiction emerged in the same manner that Henry James explained the "germ" or origin of his fiction. Taken as a whole, the correspondence focuses on two major issues: "invention" and concern for biography as it affects "invention." In the exchange an esthetic emerges which challenges many of the easy biographical assumptions that have been made about Hemingway's novels and short stories, and Cowley's perceptive challenges to Hemingway provide an explanation of how, in great writers, invention proceeds primarily from knowledge. There has frequently been an assumption that Hemingway's desire to protect his private life was actually a cover-up for criminal or sexual activities better left unspecified. A number of Hemingway's own comments about his military and private life give some basis for these suspicions. What emerges from the correspondence with Cowley is an entirely different foundation for Hemingway's wish to protect his early life. At the very least this new view deserves to be given equal weight with the earlier one. At stake is a theory about the sources of Hemingway's fiction.

Hemingway referred to the process of writing fiction out of experience and other knowledge as "invention."[7] What Hemingway meant by "invention" will emerge from his use of the word, but it should be understood here that it was closely linked to the classical definition of *inventio* as recorded by Cicero in *De Inventione*: "taking care for the matter," as distinct from "elocution," which was "taking care for the words and style." Hemingway had no fears at the time of this correspondence about his ability to handle the words and style. The "matter" and the topics he wanted to write about out of his own experience, however, were of deep concern to him. Primarily, this concern resulted from the fact that there were very few incidents that he wanted to write about out of his past and that as time passed it was always more difficult for him to keep them accurately in his mind. This led to his fear that inaccurate biographies would only make it more difficult for him to remember "what really happened." For Hemingway, as for Cicero, a sharp recollection of incidents was the first step of successful "invention."

Accurate recall was important because Hemingway was aware that not all of his stories came from his personal experience. Some stories were based on his reading or were expansions of tales told to him by friends in Upper Michigan, Paris, or Italy during World War I. In his correspondence with Cowley he distinguished carefully between *A Farewell to Arms*, which was an "entirely made-up novel,"[8] and "In Another Country" and "A Way You'll Never Be," which were related to him by other people.[9] Hemingway's distinction between the two categories reveals the necessity for keeping an accurate account of his own experience.

Hemingway's lifelong quarrel with the press was caused primarily by his attempt to maintain this distinction. The more he read about himself, the less he knew about himself. Allegations, gossip, casual contempt, critical jealousy, and the false photographic image presented in the popular press contributed not only to the public's misconception of Hemingway but, more importantly, to Hemingway's conception of himself.[10] Edmund Wilson was typical of those who embraced the popular image presented in the popular press:

> Bunny Wilson's whole theory that I started out to publicize myself as a hunter and fisherman by pictures, etc., is truly false. Max Perkins was always after me for pictures. I was always hunting and fishing ever since I can remember, and the only times we took pictures were then. You don't take pictures looking at Mantegna, Piero del Ia Francesca, Giotto, learning Spanish, French, navigation, English, aerodynamics or inside the Prado, the Luxemburg, the Jeu de Paume or the Louvre. You wouldn't tolerate anybody interrupting your working, taking pictures, but inevitably when you win events, set records, etc., or have a fine trophy someone takes pictures.[11]

Hemingway's list of activities that occupied his time when no one was standing by with a camera has escaped critical attention until very recently. The list itself reveals the triviality of much of the biographical criticism written about Hemingway and why he objected to it.

In addition to the circulation of misinformation, all of the biographical enquiries wasted a great deal of Hemingway's time:

> That's why I don't want any biography. Literary, yes. I have written it and stand by it, but unless I checked on everything and told you what was true

and what was false you would run into all kinds of shit, printed as well as verbal.

> Also it is bad for me. Makes me think about my-self instead of about writing which is what I should do. I should write and if I am ever dead then people can write about life. But while alive, I should be a writer and the hell with anything else.[12]

Continual intrusion into his personal and public life by Baker, Fenton,[13] Young, Max Eastman, and Edmund Wilson,[14] among others, caused him no end of anger and confusion.

When Cowley was commissioned by *Life* magazine to write a feature article on Hemingway, he joined the group of biographers who were intruding on Hemingway's domain. As part of the agreement, *Life* offered to pay Cowley's expenses for a trip to Havana to interview Hemingway, and Cowley could not resist the opportunity. Hemingway was immediately cooperative,[15] although suspicious, and invited Cowley to Havana, suggesting that he stay at the *Ambos Mundos Hotel*. Hemingway also advised Cowley to contact General "Buck" Lanham if he wanted to get "the straight dope" on the role Hemingway played in the war. Cowley, his wife, Muriel, and his son, Rob, spent two weeks in Havana during February of 1948.[16] Hemingway and Cowley got on very well together. Cowley reported that they "got drunk together and exchanged confidences (none of which went into the profile)."[17] When the correspondence resumed after Cowley's return to Connecticut, he began to ask questions about information collected both in Cuba and from General Lanham. Among other matters, the letters that followed concerned "very bad trouble" in Italy,[18] the Rambouillet affair,[19] Hemingway's activities off the Cuban coast during 1943-44, and Hemingway's World War I wounds. These were uncomfortable episodes in Hemingway's life, and he wanted to make certain that Cowley would not violate any confidences exchanged during their meetings in Havana. Moreover, he clearly wanted to write about some of the incidents himself, and he was beginning to suspect that Cowley would have to be added to his growing list of intruding meddlers. Owing to Cowley's impeccable taste, and his decision not to violate any personal confidences, Cowley and Hemingway remained good friends and continued their correspondence for many years.

Cowley had shown an unusual measure of sympathy for Hemingway's concern for biography, and Hemingway was generally appreciative of the fact that Cowley was primarily interested in his works. Cowley had to walk a fairly narrow line between Hemingway and the editors of *Life* in order to get the portrait published, but when Thomas Bledsoe, an editor at Rinehart, asked Cowley to read Philip Young's manuscript for a new book, Cowley was barely able to manage the balancing act required. On the one hand, Cowley defended the book to Hemingway, arguing that Young might as well go ahead since he would be able to manage some control over him. On the other hand, if Hemingway prohibited Young's manuscript from being published, someone else would do a similar book and then neither of them would have any control. Control was necessary because Cowley mistrusted Young's confusion of Hemingway with the heroes of his novels.[20] Cowley felt he could correct the manuscript sufficiently so that both Hemingway and Bledsoe would be satisfied. Young and Bledsoe were not impressed, however, and eventually Hemingway became furious with Cowley for tolerating the whole business. Cowley's insistence that someone was going to do the job anyway carried little weight with Hemingway. Eventually Cowley tried to extricate himself, but he always found that his loyalty to Hemingway required that he try to mediate and bring pressure to bear on the editors at Rinehart.

An earlier incident stemming from the *Life* portrait had made Hemingway exasperated with Cowley, and his implication in the Young book sounded like a rerun of the old problems with the Life article. The earlier incident had involved Oak Park, which always made Hemingway angry. Cowley had it all wrong; Hemingway tried to set him straight about parts of the *Life* article:

> I know how good and friendly and careful you were in that piece just as I know there are lots of things you don't know and things people told you that weren't straight and plenty things I didn't tell you. Other things you draw out a strange interpretation from like not going to dances. Do you know

how that works? My older sister was not popular until her last year in school and then only with the jerks. I was not allowed to ask any girl I liked to any formal dances until my sister had been asked. Was in reserve as her escort. All girls you would want to ask are asked a long time ahead. Marg would be asked about the last two or three days before the dance. No girls you were fond of left by then and I would say the Hell with it.[21]

In spite of Cowley's misinterpretation of some data, Hemingway was actually flattered by Cowley's idea that he would like to expand the *Life* portrait into a full-length biography, but he ended the discussion of the *Life* article by writing:

I truly think that we suffer in our times from an exaggerated emphasis on personality and I would much rather have my work discussed than the offence of my life. It is OK to have a record of what you have done and it should be made before the people who know what has happened are dead. But I think that it is very bad for the man involved and could be extremely bad for his writing if he ever started to think of himself as a character rather than simply someone trying to write a story as well as he can. I am afraid that I may be stuffy or righteous in expressing this so please forgive me if there is any stuffiness or righteousness or chicken in this attitude.[22]

This controversy over the Young book went on for many letters and finally Cowley had to give in and admit, "I wish to God I had never seen the Philip Young manuscript. It has got me into the damndest hippocritic, hypocitic and hypocritical situation . . . . This is my last will and testament on the subject, signed Malcolm Cowley, so help me God, Amen."[23] This was the end of Cowley's projected biography of Hemingway.

All of Hemingway's fears on the subject of biography were exacerbated as he watched with some horror what Arthur Mizener was doing to F. Scott Fitzgerald. What happened to "poor Scott" could also happen to him. Ultimately, Mizener did a job on Fitzgerald, Hemingway wrote to Mizener, which compared favorably with the job the undertaker had done on Hemingway's father's face after he had shot himself. "One remembers the face better as it actually was. But the undertaker pleases those who come to the funeral."[24] As part of his research into Fitzgerald's life, Mizener initiated a substantial correspondence with Hemingway which ran from July 6, 1949, to January 11, 1951, and which included eight letters from Hemingway to Mizener. *The Far Side of Paradise* was published in 1950, and an article based on Mizener's research appeared in *Life* in January of 1951.[25] Although Fitzgerald was already dead, Hemingway's concern for biographical intrusion was heightened by what Mizener had done to his one-time friend. "Mizener's shameful performance in *Life*,"[26] Hemingway wrote to Cowley, was based on what Hemingway called "grave robbery":

> Mizener deceived me completely by his letters. I thought he was a straight guy and then came that unspeakable piece of grave robbery he wrote for Life. When a man and a fellow writer has a daughter married and with children living to hang a heritage of insanity into them for money, seems hardly a Christian act. Poor Scott!![27]

Mizener had quoted freely from personal letters which Scott had written to and about Zelda and their daughter, and Hemingway obviously could not see what any of it had to do with an understanding of Fitzgerald's work. When Mizener ended his Life article with an assumption that biography was the major source of fiction and proved his point by quoting Malcolm Cowley, Hemingway felt he had to be careful lest his letters and conversations with Cowley would be treated in the same way.[28]

The distasteful intrusion of the critic into the personal affairs of Fitzgerald resulted in a totally false impression of the writer. Hemingway complained that both Cowley and Edmund Wilson had tried to turn Fitzgerald into the Henry James of the 1920s.[29] This was too much for Hemingway, especially since Fitzgerald couldn't even spell "Hemingway":

He couldn't be blamed for misspelling my name. He couldn't spell anything, and that spelling is a complicated social problem; two "m's" means "bastard." Hemingway means "silk company" and such a long name as Hemingway was really asking too damn much of Scott.[30]

> As any reader of the Hemingway-Mizener correspondence knows, Hemingway had a great admiration for Fitzgerald both as a friend and as a writer with "golden talent." His reservations were based on the distinction between invention and knowledge. Cowley had earned Hemingway's suspicion by reediting *Tender Is the Night*;[31]

Hemingway felt that Fitzgerald's first published version was far better than Cowley's reedited text. Hemingway received the reedited version on November 19, 1951. The next day he was ready for Cowley:

> Truly I did not want the reforms to turn out as I was afraid they might, but I'm afraid the whole idea was just a bad idea of Scott's. In the straight chronological order the book loses the magic completely. Starting off with a case history there is no secret to discover and no mystery and all sense of a seemingly magical world (the world of Sara and Gerald Muphy) being destroyed by someone that is unknown and lost. By the time the bathroom incident goes off the reader knows everything which was to come as a shock. In the form it is now it is simply a pathological [sic] and not a nice one at that. It has all the dullness of all the stories of the insane and where it had the charm of the strange mixture that was Scott it is now about as much fun to read as The Snake Pit. I know you did it for Scott and it was what he wanted, but I think if he had been completely sane I would have argued him out of it. It is just like taking the wings off a butterfly and arranging them so he can fly straight as a bee flies

and losing all of that dust that makes the colors that make the butterfly magical in the process.[32]

Readers of *A Moveable Feast* will recall the butterfly metaphor for Fitzgerald in the headnote to section 17:

> His talent was as natural as the pattern that was made by the dust on a butterfly's wing. At this time he understood it no more than the butterfly did and he did not know when it was brushed or marred. Later he became conscious of his damaged wings and of their construction and he learned to think and could not fly any more because the love of flight was gone and he could only think of when it had been effortless.[33]

The manuscript of this published version in the John F. Kennedy Library reveals the more sober and critical view that Hemingway actually held on Fitzgerald in a sentence eliminated by the editors from the published edition: "He even needed professionals or normally educated people to make his writing legible and not illiterate."[34] As Hemingway wrote Cowley, Fitzgerald was one of "the worst educated writers who ever wrote prose,"[35] and worse, Cowley was one of those who had perpetuated what Hemingway considered to be a false image of the writer.[36] Clearly, Fitzgerald had little knowledge to build on after his meteoric rise to fame.[37]

When Cowley edited the new version of *Tender Is the Night* according to notes left by Fitzgerald, Hemingway was annoyed because he felt that Cowley did for Fitzgerald what Max Perkins had done for Thomas Wolfe. As a result, both writers had been credited with knowledge and skill which they did not possess:

> "But Malcolm, what do you really think of all this editing of writers? For instance, what would Wolfe be if they let him publish as he wrote it and corrected it himself? Shouldn't the books have been by Thomas Wolfe and Maxwell Perkins? Now Scott comes out tidied properly by you and knowing both French and

Italian in both of which languages he was completely comical."[38]

Hemingway reminisces about a time when writers knew something:

> Wasn't there ever a time when a writer wrote, re-wrote, corrected his punctuation and spelling and decided himself what his characters were going to do? Now it seems to me to be like the two platoon system in football. Are we to look forward to when they have offensive and defensive writers? It seems sort of comic to me. Charlie Scribner told me that several of his authors do not even read their proofs. No wonder writing is going on the bum. Charlie put someone over my proofs before they were returned to me. The going over consisted in querying place names which the go-over had not been able to locate in a Rand-McNalley [sic] atlas. He could find no Fossalta di Piave. Thought because Monastir was in Serbia there could not be one in Venito. He said only Fornaci was on the Po River. Of course Fossalta means a town built behind a sunken road. There are hundreds of them, but only one is famous. Monastir is spelled three different ways. Fornaci is a town or village where there is a furnace or lime kiln.

> I had to explain all that. But the editor would have changed them because those reference points on the military map one to ten thousand were not in the Rand-McNalley [sic] atlas. Now maybe I misspelled McNalley in a letter. But in galley-proofs I would look it up or accept the corrections of a proofreader. But ninety per cent of the corrections of proofreaders I have to strike out. When I first started with Scribners, eliminating the interference with my punctuation and sentence structure by proofreaders was a lot of work. I got very angry and told Max they would have to

stop fooling with my galleys. I told him to have them put question marks on anything they did not understand and if it was as I meant it to be I would rub out their question marks and he could believe that was how I wanted it. I want to be checked on the use of the apostrophe and on any obviously misspelled words or printer's errors, but at the start honest to christ proof readers used to try to fix your stuff up the way they would have written it.[39]

When Hemingway read Cowley's defense of his version of *Tender Is the Night*, he was even more critical. Attention to detail had escaped both Fitzgerald and Cowley. Hemingway decided to set them straight:

Errors: relizing for realizing on page 194. Cavear with an e for caviar (this spelling is obsolete and is a bastard one at best, but is used throughout), also you can't see Valais at night, described as a short way out of Zurich. There are other small things you will catch in any future edition and if you want to spell caviar as cavear that is a question of taste. It is legal.

None of the above is important unless everything is important in writing, but truly I think the changing about of material is.[40]

The relationship with Fitzgerald was a long and difficult one for Hemingway. As much as he admired Fitzgerald, he knew that Fitzgerald did not take care of his talent.[41] Alcoholism was only one of the aspects of mismanagement, and he always saw his own career as being perilously close to Scott's. Hemingway knew that he personally did not have the charm that saved Fitzgerald,[42] but what his comments on Fitzgerald and Cowley's version of *Tender Is the Night* make clear is that Hemingway felt that he himself did have the knowledge and a sense of invention that were necessary for a good writer. He guarded these qualities ruthlessly. He knew they were what separated him from most other writers, and he did not want them jeopardized by meddling critics, arrogant editors and proofreaders, or his own failure to recognize what knowledge he actually had and from which he could invent. In the final analysis, it was Fitzgerald's career that taught him so much, that made him so suspicious of biographical criticism, and that forced him to protect what made invention possible. As Hemingway wrote to Cowley, it was the confusion of invention and knowledge that had worked so hard against his friend Scott:

> Scott caught the surface in the people that he knew or met with a fine brightness, but he always used to interrogate everybody. "Did you sleep with your wife before you were married?" I've heard him ask that to someone the first time he met them. How could he expect to get the truth that way?.... ..

> There are writers to whom people come all their lives and tell things that writers would give everything not to know. But he hears them and never uses them except as the knowledge he invents from. But Scott would mix up as in *Tender Is the Night* himself and Zelda with Gerald and Sara and they were very different. He got balled up inventing from mixtures of opposites in people instead of inventing from his knowledge of people themselves.[43]

In addition to giving Hemingway perspective on Fitzgerald's career, Hemingway's concept of invention from knowledge had very definite positive implications for his own work. Although there are numerous references to the process throughout the letters, particularly as they apply to other writers, it was the publication of The Old Man and the Sea[44] that resulted in a spirited exchange between Hemingway and Cowley and that allowed Hemingway to give Cowley a lecture on just what invention was all about.

The spirited exchange was initiated by Cowley about a year earlier while he was reading Jay Leyda's *The Melville Log*.[45] On this occasion Cowley was responding to Hemingway's accusation that he had given Fitzgerald a credibility that he did not deserve. Cowley was sensitive on the point. In defending his own version, he recalled Melville's reaction to his editors. In a long and fascinating passage Cowley reviewed the entries in the Log that parallel many aspects of Hemingway's strictures:

> I had been reading a big collection of documents called The Melville Log in which Melville's life is recorded from day to day. So far as the records survive. His daughter Fanny hated him and burned most of the family papers so that people thought for a long time there weren't any records at all. But the scholars have been working on them for the last twenty years and now they've collected so many documents that merely to quote the pertinent pages from them makes up a two-volume work of 933 pages. In November 1851 Melville had finished Moby Dick. He had written it in a little more than a year; written it twice in a high state of elation but after he finished it he was dead tired, morose, suicidal, then without giving himself a chance for rest he plunged into Pierre. Worked on it from eight o'clock to dark each day in a cold room in Pittsfield, didn't eat until he staggered out of the room in the dusk. It was a crazy book when he finished it and was such a complete failure (362 copies sold in twenty years) that he was never again able to earn a living as a writer. He had himself a long breakdown, stopped seeing his friends, tried to earn a living as a magazine writer but failed at it, tried to earn a living as a lecturer but failed at it, finally gave up the writing game completely (he was trying to learn to be a poet, some of his poems were very good but he regarded that as a private matter); got a job in a customs house at $5.00 a day and lived in retirement for thirty years, then other writers who admired him, there were a few, looked him up in his retirement. He gave them the brush-off and apparently most of his family came to regard him as a mean old man.[46]

Cowley concludes the long recitation of Melville's woe with reference to Melville's text: "He had no education beyond age twelve, or no education but the very best, the sort to be had by shipping before the mast. He read enormously. He couldn't spell and his grammar was shaky but his sisters used to copy his manuscripts for him in those days before the typewriter and they peppered the text with commas and changed don't to doesn't. But later when his wife copied his manuscripts he taught her not to use any punctuation whatever. He put it all in himself in the final revision."[47] Cowley had patiently recounted the whole Melville situation so that he could set up his own theory about editing:

> So we're back at the big question. How much should an editor do? I think it all depends whose manuscript he is working on. When a writer knows what he wants to do then the editor should keep his hands off the manuscript strictly and the copy reader and the proofreader should confine themselves to queries and questions of spelling. When a writer is worth publishing like our late friend Lil Abner [Wolfe], but doesn't know when to stop then an editor like Max Perkins can certainly help him (and help the public more by saving them the trouble of reading packing boxes full of tripe). Scott's a different matter. Generally speaking he knew what he wanted in a big way and in small ways too, but he was always running into trouble about questions of spelling, especially proper names. He called you Himinway and always misspelled the name of Ginevra King with whom he had been in love for three years desperately. He called her Genevra. Grammar, geography, chronology is when a man named McKibben in Tender "unscrewed two bloody wire hairs from a nearby table and departed." On the next page he was still there, still talking. He hadn't any theory about those details, he just wanted them to be conventionally right and hadn't the sort of eye that caught them on the page. For some damn reason he never put the book through Scribner's copy-

editing department where those matters would have been caught and queried. He simply turned it over to Miss what's-her-name, his nice secretary, to handle. Scott himself got a Frenchman to fix up the French quotations, though a couple must have slipped past the Frenchman, but had no help on the Italian. What I did to the book was just what Scribner's proofreading department would have done if the manuscript had passed through their hands. I thought it was the only fair thing to do for Scott because otherwise people were privileged to think that he was the only illiterate author in the United States. They ought to see some other manuscripts. People like you who work over every detail of the manuscript are rare as hell in the country these days. They are the last individual handicraftsman. Most of our so-called writers just do part of their work as if they had only one job on the production line before the manuscript moves into the varnish room.[48]

Hemingway's reply is swift.[49] His sympathy is immediate for Melville. Melville, for Hemingway, knew something that those around him and later the scholars (he returns in this letter to the buzzard image for the critics and adds the hyena for good measure) did not. The key word is "knew." Cowley's implied compliment in the comparison did not stop Hemingway from establishing his own criteria. In one sense Hemingway's reply is a restatement of the "iceberg" theory of *Death in the Afternoon*, but here he is more precise about what it means. Beneath the surface of his short novel lies a foundation of knowledge, Hemingway insisted, that neither Scott nor Faulkner could manage and which constitutes that seven-eighths that lies beneath the surface.[50] It is not sufficient that a certain part of the plot stick up above the surface, leaving the reader free to imagine a fund of possibilities and probabilities beneath. What is fundamental for Hemingway is that what is beneath the surface is a foundation of information and knowledge which informs every word he chooses to expose.[51] Hemingway's theory was best stated by Henry James in his famous dialogue with Walter Besant. Considering the plight of the young novelist, James struck a balance between experience and knowledge: "The power to guess the unseen from the seen, to trace the implication of things, to judge the whole piece by the pattern, the condition of feeling life in general so completely that you are well on your way to knowing any particular corner of it this cluster of gifts may almost be said to constitute experience."[52] For James and for Hemingway, invention is not simply a matter of personal experience recollected in tranquility or passion. It is what emerges when a person tries to be "one of the people on whom nothing is lost." A novel must have a "truth of detail" that rises above all other characteristics. That is, in fact, "the supreme virtue of the novel" and the singular "merit on which all [the novel's] other merits helplessly and submissively depend." This process whereby knowledge informs experience is at the heart of James's essay and labels precisely what Cowley and Hemingway were writing to each other about. Knowing, therefore, was an obsession with Hemingway.

Knowing about people, knowing the competition of other writers, knowing about war, fish, witchcraft—the list is endless. Hemingway always returned to the same theme: "I just tried to invent from what I know .... I try to invent as straight as what I have known."[53] The first thing, of course, was to know.

His library shows that his thirst for knowledge was insatiable.[54] According to those who knew him best, he was constantly reading and attempting to expand the fund from which he could invent.

One of the many writers who according to Hemingway failed to combine knowledge with experience was Norman Mailer. Hemingway was critical of the experience that Mailer brought to the craft of writing; he felt that Mailer's knowledge of warfare was particularly thin. *The Naked and the Dead* (1949), he wrote to Cowley, was "so phony it couldn't hold the pace. Full of frustrated sadism and all combat faked." Hemingway recognized Mailer as a skillful writer who had produced "several good passages based on at least one patrol and there was some evidence that he had been a general's aid, but not for long." What particularly bothered Hemingway was the "General giving coordinates off map without looking at map."[55] The whole scene lost credibility for Hemingway because the general assigned coordinates 439.56 and 440.06 from "a mental image of his battle map."[56] Hemingway concluded that Mailer had been on the scene only a short while. He admits:

> Mailer may be a very good writer. Is certainly skillful as hell and it is a much better book than Three Soldiers. But since when do they split up a patrol to take back a mortally wounded (gut shot and dying before they picked him up) man and have him die for two hundred pages. C'est pornagraphique. Mais, c'nest ce pas la guerre .... I felt all the time I was reading a book by an infant *protegé* who had read everything.[57]

Invention from knowledge, therefore, had to be based on extensive knowledge of the subject, but also had to be filtered through a writer who had experience. The rest is pornography. Early in August 1952, after reading an advance copy of *The Old Man and the Sea*, Cowley wrote to Hemingway:

> The Old Man and the Sea is pretty marvelous. The old man is marvelous and the sea is too and so is the fish. I'm proud of them all and of you and glad that I am reviewing the book for the Herald Tribune. As yet I don't know what I am going to say because I'm getting a lot of space to write about such a short book, but it will be a pleasant task to fill the space. Maybe among other things I can talk about your prose which has that quality here as elsewhere of being absolutely fresh with the words standing out separately on the pages, as if nobody before had ever used the simple words of the English language. And to point up what you do in that story, I can talk about the present rage for symbols and myths, and the kids saying, "Go to," I will use symbols "go to," I will create the myth, and all of them forgetting that if a character doesn't live it, it can't be a myth. So you give us a character and a story, and the reader is privileged to read them whatever symbolic or mythical qualities they suggest to him.

But, meanwhile, the characters in the story have their own life.[58]

Hemingway was, of course, flattered by Cowley's use of the term "myth." He responded by explaining what he knew and how all of it went into the background of writing about in The Art of Sea . Hemingway's reply is a twentieth-century recounting of how Henry James was writing Fiction:

I'm glad it is short. If I wanted to I could have put in that everybody lived on the same road, and what they did and what they thought. And how they lived and how they put in the dinghy race and bootlegging days and revolution and civil, medical and religious trouble and every change in death and marriage and birth and economic thing I know about the village and the time we killed the whale (sperm) and the time we caught the whale shark and Gregario's five daughters and the time we found gold down at the cove and my girl Smokey was in love with me since she was nine and always sat on the seawall to watch our boat come in and didn't let me know about it un-til she was seventeen, and all that stuff that make up what you call a novel. Maybe you can do it better. But it has been done well and life is short, no matter how long it is. And why should you do what had already been done well? Especially, if there is something else that you have been working for since the chapters in the first in our time. This story, Malcolm, is what I knew and had figured out in those early chapters with what I have learned since. When I wrote those I had learned that when I read novels I would read one part or section or incident in the whole novel that truly convinced me and made me feel that I had been there. But they were always wrapped in these layers of writing and rhetoric and all and I tried to write those chapters to get down the inner true thing. They weren't exercises. I always wrote everything as though it were all and everything I would ever write. But when I wrote this Old Man and the Sea, I knew more and I could write with the same degree of concentration and elimination, and tell what the kids, as you say, call the myth, but making it a simple, straight and believable story. You see they cannot have a myth without having a hero. A hero has to face things no one else can face. Things have to be unbelievable to make a myth, but they have to be made absolutely believable. Now in our time, the hero has to be made believable too. He has to be someone who has suffered and been defeated. You start out with him on a day when he has been defeated 84 times straight. That seems unbelievable, if it is really true, and you make it perfectly believable. You make him an absolutely believable man. Then as he moves out into the sea, which is an unbelievable place, you make it soundly believable. To do what he has to do you have to show how he has been a great man and a champion, and you make that unbelievable. Combat with the Negro from Cienfuegos (which was true) becomes believable. But what the hell? You said all this in your first paragraph. But it is hard not to talk matter when I have no one to talk it with.[59]

Cowley had expanded his own comment on myth in the context of their earlier discussion of Melville. He continued his letter by expanding their earlier exchange on Melville:

There is a curious contrast with Moby Dick, when the whole comes to stand for the impersonal power and malignity of Nature. Your fish and your fisherman are equally parts of Nature. "Brothers" as the old man says. Each of them plays his assigned role as in a ritual drama. The old man loves and honors the fish and one suspects that the fish loves and honors the old man. And in the end, the fish and man have collaborated (like bull and matador) to make life on this planet seem more dramatic than it was before their battle started.[60]

As Hemingway considered this flattering analogy and comment on the mythological dimensions of his new novel, he responded to the Melville contrast with a notation focusing on his visual concept of what he had been writing about. He revealed a knowledge not only of the sea and the character he was writing about but of how the sea appeared in art:

> That thing you speak about of Melville and the malignity of Nature is interesting because in the other books I try to show, never having thought of that, that the sea is a puta [whore], but she is our mother. The whole conception of the malignity of Nature always seems to me to belong to those Dore [Paul Gustave Dore, 1832?-83] illustrations. I can remember in some of the other books where the boys were arguing about the ocean. How she did nothing wrong. It was always the things that were done to her, the way they were done to a woman by the moon and the winds. She traps you by seeming so fair and attractive, but you are a fool if you are trapped.[61]

Hemingway was very close here to chapter 42 of *Moby-Dick*, "The Whiteness of the Whale," where Melville meditates on the union of purity and beauty and terror inherent in the color white. Hemingway's use of "seeming," perhaps Melville's favorite word (the whale only "seemed" white), suggests a closeness and an appreciation for Melville that went beyond the parallel use of a marlin and a whale. Hemingway's choice of the great fish had not been taken casually. He continued to develop the background of his short novel for Cowley: "Once I thought I would like to write about whales. I've ironed four sperm whale, and lost them and killed one. But Melville wrote about whales and whaling was a wonderful thing then. But I'm not sure he really loved them, although he went whaling and he certainly studied them."[62] Since whaling and whales were no longer a part of Hemingway's time, he felt he could not have made the relationship meaningful. As he gently questioned Melville's relationship to whales,

Hemingway carefully explained to Cowley the difference between his own concept of the sea and the world of whaling that surrounded Melville:

> But I promise you the relationship as it grows, be-
> tween the old man and the fish, is not a false one. Nor
> is anything the old man did impossible nor some-
> thing that has been done by other people. I am so
> happy that you like it, and if you have to wander off
> about prose, there is little to wander off about that
> the boys don't know, just as there is a lot that could
> be in this story that I did not put in to keep it to the
> old sound proportions of the iceberg; one-eighth that
> shows and seven-eighths underwater to give it bal-
> ance.[63]

One aside by Cowley gives a measure of his desire to help Hemingway and his genuine esteem for the man. They had had many exchanges about editing, and Cowley, unable to resist his professional background, adds almost as a postscript: "The albacore on page 43-44 turns into a bonito on page 64 when the old man eats him."[64] This is a casual comment in a paragraph on other matters concerning the story. Hemingway was not amused:

> It is all right about the bonito; actually the fish
> could be any one of three. But the fishermen call
> them all bonito, and when he was tired, the old man
> would think of it by the shortest name. They are all
> canned and packed under the one name "bonito" and
> none of the three is the fish they call the bonito from
> Florida north. It's okay, I checked the reference and
> the transferring on page 44, bottom of the page, and
> 62-63-64. Thanks for mentioning it though, maybe
> I should have explained it, but when he said, "alba-
> cora" he meant that he judged it to be that type of
> fish which they generically call "bonito." That doesn't
> even hold all the way around the island, because some
> fishermen have Canary Island ancestry, (like the old
> man). And others come from the Balearics or from

Catalonia. And still others from Galicia. And the
Basque country and a few from Asturias. My point
is that when he caught him he would classify him as
a special type of "Bonito" and when he was tired, he
would just be a "bonito."[65]

In the margin, Hemingway added in his own hand, "This fish was
a small tuna, but the old man being from the Canaries, would call
him 'albacore' and think of him generally as "Bonito."" The point here
is not whether the information Hemingway produces is accurate as
far as the classification of fish in Cuban waters is concerned, but how
important it was to him that what shows above the surface of the
story rest on knowledge below the surface. But Hemingway was not
finished:

> If I made the fish so he is seen and felt by the read-
> er, then my responsibility ends as long as I have the
> old man speak of him properly, or as he would speak.
> If the reader has erudition everything is there for him
> to use it on, but if I start hitting him with erudition,
> then it is almost as bad as using footnotes in a story. I
> would have to then explain that broad-billed sword-
> fish are called "bonito" off Peru and Chile, while they
> are known as "Imperador" off Cuba, and "Pez Espa-
> da" off Spain. And then we would be explaining the
> differences between broadbill and marlin which no-
> body agrees on yet, etc.[66]

Hemingway is no doubt becoming somewhat tedious, but
the point of Cowley's comment is that it questions Hemingway's
knowledge rather than merely pointing out a copy editor's slip.[67]
Hemingway did not drop the idea of erudition lest Cowley had not
understood his earlier treatise on "bonito":

> I think you should know all this and much more
> when you write a story. Erudition shouldn't show.
> You know Ezra [Pound] can't leave any erudition
> true or false out of a poem and what the results are
> sometime. Ideally a man should know everything,

but when he writes [he should] make something so that it will really happen to the reader; be made (not described); so that afterwards the reader will have had the experience; not seen it or heard about it; then he cannot clutter at all.[68]

It is this use of the word "made" (not described) that is the key to Hemingway's technique, as outlined in these letters to Cowley. Knowledge of all the variations of bonito is as necessary for the writer as knowledge of the muscles beneath the skin is necessary for the classical sculptor. The knowledge that lay beneath invention was as solid and necessary as the cones, cylinders, and cubes beneath Cezanne's mountains and apples. Neither Cezanne nor Hemingway could paint the surface or "make a scene" without the knowledge of what lay beneath.[69]

Cowley apparently never answered this remarkable letter, but when his review of *The Old Man and the Sea* appeared in *The New York Herald Tribune*,[70] it was clearly based on their exchange. Cowley used the differences between Hemingway's novel and Moby-Dick as structure for the review. After making a passing reference to what had become known as "the poor man's Moby-Dick," Cowley was quick to focus on the differences between the two novels. He saw the new short novel as a classic (a work that accepts "limitations of space, subject and treatment while trying to achieve faultlessness within the limitations") but carefully showed the distance between the two novels as Hemingway had explained them to him a month earlier. *Moby-Dick* had accepted no limits, was certainly not short, and was essentially romantic in its portrayal of Ahab as a Titan in search of the unattainable. Cowley continued:

Hemingway's hero is an old man reduced to living on food that is begged or stolen for him by a young boy .... Although he goes out further than anyone, there is no sense that God is immanent in nature because when the man prays, he addresses a transcendent God. Both Hemingway's old man and the marlin are in nature: "they are even brothers in nature."[71]

Moreover, they are equals, and the strength of one is matched against the intelligence of the other. Following Hemingway's lead, Cowley insisted that *The Old Man and the Sea* was as different from *Moby-Dick* as anything ever written.

The second focus of Cowley's review was Hemingway's language and its relation to classic constraint, simplicity, and concentration:

> There is no attempt in it [*The Old Man and the Sea*] to express the inexpressible by inventing new words and turns of phrases; instead Hemingway uses the oldest and shortest words, the simplest constructions, but gives these new value—as if English were a strange language that he had studied or invented for himself and was trying to write in its original purity.[72]

Cowley continues by analyzing a short passage, finding in it what Hemingway told him to find, and ends with a personal aside which reveals his correspondence with Hemingway and which anyone who has read some of Hemingway's original letters will appreciate. He notes in his review the double and triple spaces between words in Hemingway's typical typewritten style and admits that they may come from a defective space bar: "But I like to believe that it has something to do with his feeling that each word has a special value and should stand out separately and clearly on the page. That is what the words seem to do in *The Old Man and the Sea*. The writing has the quality of being familiar and yet perpetually new that is the essence of classical prose,"[73] On Hemingway's insistence, Cowley had "read it again" and detected that the prose was a "transparent medium" for revealing the story beneath the surface. Cowley admitted that as he read *The Old Man and the Sea* again, the layers of meaning, patterns in the transparency, musical tone, and values emerged for him as solidly as "turquoise set in silver."[74]

On the basis of Cowley's praise and the generally good reception of *The Old Man and the Sea*, Hemingway felt he still had that old thing, the ability to "make" from "knowledge." He wrote Cowley:

> This new book that I have is a concentration of everything I have learned and focused on all my life,

but I hope none of that shows. But if it seems too simple, when you read it, please read it again .... But this time I have tried without one trick and yet with all the knowledge I should have acquired by now, to make something that I would stand on as I wanted to do .... It is a good lode and it hasn't run out and when it has faulted, we have always been able to tap it again. And it will last as long as I will, and I want to last forever.[75]

Hemingway seems to have gained confidence from his correspondence with Cowley. Shortly after their correspondence ended Hemingway wrote to Charles Poore at *The New York Times* about the sources of his work and how he saw himself as working in the manner of Tolstoi:

Remember Charlie in the first war all I did mostly was hear guys talk; especially in hospital and convalescing. Their experiences get to be more vivid than your own. You invent from your own and from all of theirs. The country you know, also the weather. Then you have a map 1/50,000 for the whole front or sector; 1/15,000 if you can get one for close. Then you invent from other people's experience and knowledge and what you know yourself.

Then some son of a bitch will come along and prove you were not at that particular fight. Fine. Dr. Tolstoi was at Sevastopol. But not at Borodino. He wasn't in business in those days. But he could invent from knowledge we all were at some damned Sevastopol.[76]

Here is the most forceful statement of Hemingway's contempt for biographers. The biographers made assumptions that were downright false and demeaning to literary craftsmanship. Seldom did they have any sense of a writer's knowledge. They not only made invention difficult but destroyed the fundamental possibility of invention and its ultimate imaginative excitement.

Five days after "the man with blunderbuss" had lost his battle with "the jackals of the mind" Cowley wrote to Conrad Aiken:

> I mourn for Hemingway. He could be as mean as cat piss and as sweet as a ministering angel. It's hard to think that so much vitality, vanity, unflagging zest, eagerness to excel in everything, willingness to learn and study and finally teach everything, ability to participate in other people's lives—that all this should simply vanish. Sometime I'll tell you some of the curious things I found out about him that he didn't want the world to know.[77]

What was still important to Cowley was that Hemingway himself "knew" and that from what he knew he had been able to "invent."

Chapter 5

"CHRIST, I WISH I COULD PAINT": THE CORRESPONDENCE BETWEEN ERNEST HEMINGWAY AND BERNARD BERENSON

Hemingway's lonely life in Cuba has been generally ignored by biographers. Even Baker's biography (1969) treated almost two decades of Hemingway's life with the scantest references, and today it remains by and large a mystery. Baker's edition of only a small portion of the letters (1981) filled in some of the details, but the letters to Hemingway are, of course, omitted, and many of them are in locations not readily accessible to scholars or the interested public. Recently some details have emerged. Hemingway's support of Dr. Fidel Castro and the Cuban revolution[1] and his close association with Jose Luis Herrera Sotolongo[2] reveal the Cuban resident as more involved in Cuban affairs than earlier commentary would suggest. Most touching perhaps was his long-standing correspondence with Bernard Berenson, an authority on Renaissance art, who served Hemingway as a surrogate father with whom he occasionally differed, but whose approval Hemingway desperately needed. That correspondence, which began in 1949 and ended in 1956 shortly before Berenson's death, reveals not only a great deal about Hemingway's intellectual activity during the Cuban years, but suggests another dimension of the depression that preceded his death.

With a tone hovering somewhere between blasphemy and devotion reminiscent of e. e. cummings' young boy reflecting on the "defunct" Buffalo Bill ("Jesus/ he was a handsome man") Hemingway's exclamation to Berenson positioned him somewhere between the almost religious confidence that he could "make a scene" as well as any painter and the unsettling knowledge that critics and biographers had not noticed the parallel. "Christ, I wish I could paint"[3] was not an idle crumb tossed to Bernard Berenson, the world authority on Italian Renaissance art, but a passionate plea that someone would understand what he was trying to do. At times the humorous, tender, and affectionate tone that Hemingway used to address the aging Berenson suggests that Hemingway may have found the father he never had. At this stage in his life, biographers had bothered him unmercifully, and he was more aware than ever that they didn't have the slightest clue about the relationship between his art and his life. Perhaps the art critic would understand, or, at least, serve as a surrogate "father confessor." "Biographies at 53 are shit," Hemingway wrote to Berenson in 1953. "They [the biographers] don't know. You are too proud to tell them. And they could not understand,"[4] but Hemingway obviously felt that Berenson would understand. Berenson's rather cruel rebuke of Hemingway when he refused to grant him a private audience was a serious blow to his ego at a time when he was desperately looking for someone to give meaning to his life. Miró and Cezanne had sufficed during one phase of his career, but a respected art critic who might be able to recognize that Hemingway could "make a scene" like any other painter might be the answer to his lonely paternal search of the 1950s. Ironically, Berenson's reputation now, as an art critic, is unraveling as his dubious relationship with Joseph Duveen is gradually emerging.[5] But the Berenson that Hemingway knew during his later years was a connoisseur without equal.

Nevertheless, few understood why Hemingway included Berenson among those whom he said deserved the Nobel Prize for literature more than he did. When asked for his reaction after the award was announced in 1954, Hemingway said that he would have been happier if Bernard Berenson, the art critic "who had devoted a lifetime to the most lucid and best writing on painting that has been produced" had been honored instead of him[6] . For all of his loathing of the critics and biographers, his highest admiration remained for the analytical perceptions of the art critic who had taught the world how to look at Renaissance art. Little wonder, then, that as Mary continued her gentle flirtatious correspondence with Bernard Berenson, her husband, as she said, "edged her out"[7]. If he couldn't paint, he at least wanted to talk to someone who knew what painting was all about.

This, of course, was nothing new. Although he was starved for intellectual companionship in Cuba[8], he counted many artists among his friends, and his library contained almost 200 volumes on painters and art—including seven volumes by and about Berenson (see Appendix II). As Hemingway and Berenson exchanged opinions on such painters as Velazquez and El Greco, Miró and Cezanne, Hemingway admitted that he envied painters such as Picasso[9] who could even sell their failures, unlike writers. According to Hemingway, painters were greater than writers to start with.[10] In the twilight of his life, "Christ, 1 wish I could paint," constituted not only admiration for the work of an accomplished connoisseur of Renaissance art and his admiration for many of his friends, but also an indication of the direction and intention of his own career.

Although Hemingway was aware of Berenson's reputation in the art world as early as 1928,[11'] the correspondence between them did not begin until August 25, 1949. It continued until August 24, 1957, only a few months before Berenson died. Hemingway wrote 31 letters to Berenson of which 18 are omitted from Baker's edition of the *Letters* (1981). Hemingway's letters are part of the Berenson collection housed at his former villa, "*I Tatti*," located between Fiesole and Settignano, just north of Florence, Italy.[12] The friendship resulted from a visit that Mary paid to the elder critic at his home in the company of several friends. Several of Hemingway's letters contain postscripts or other notes from Mary to Berenson. Baker eliminated Mary's contribution to the correspondence. It is a serious omission because Mary's mild flirtations encouraged Berenson's breezy compliments which helped sustain the dialogue. To document Hemingway's obvious assumption that their correspondence would eventually be published, a complete record of the correspondence list include a carefully typed letter by Mary to Berenson late in the association as it clarifies the origin, the context, and the rationale for their correspondence. The letter certainly reads like a directive to future editors.

In addition to recording that she first met Berenson in the company of the Australian journalist, Alan Moorhead and his wife, Mary Hemingway included several anecdotes that were later retold in her autobiography and that establish the warmth of her relationship to Berenson.[13] The typewritten letter is included in the Ernest Hemingway file at "*1 Tatti*", and its placement and tone certainly suggest that it was carefully prepared as an adjunct to Hemingway's letter to Berenson of March 6, 1953, in which he wrote:

> Imagine when we are both dead as snakeshit and they publish the famous Berenson-Hemingstein letters. Can I advise you about God as Claudel did to Gide? Cannot we take each other to task about something? That is what the French really love. Do we have to *rompre*? All friendships in French end with this.

At this point in his life (1953) Hemingway evidently assumed that his correspondence would be published. The fact that he signed marginalia in the critical volumes in his library at *Finca Vigia* also justifies this assumption, as does his habit of carefully dating every letter sent to Berenson.

The two men disagreed on very little, but the letters of these unlikely correspondents in their villas in out-of-the-way places revealed two strangely similar spirits lamenting the state of art in the modern world. Both men had a passion for knowledge as the foundation of art. The cultivation of connoisseurship was the *raison d'etre* of Berenson's entire life; Hemingway's passion for knowledge and accuracy in such subjects as horse racing and marlin fishing is now well documented. In addition, both men projected a charismatic presence when they entered a room; both were capable of flirtations and affairs; both were most successful in the company of women; both complained that journalists ruled the world; and both raised serious questions about the meaning of life and the utility of their own careers. They read and celebrated each other's books (see

Appendixes II and III) and, perhaps most important, both men saw and celebrated nature as if it were a work of art.

Bernard Berenson's biographer tells the story of a day in which Berenson took a friend, Iris Origo, walking above the valley of the river Sieve:

> Suddenly, B.B. stopped and, looking as fixedly as a pointer who had sighted his bird, said. "Look," pointing to a farmhouse below us, with cypresses and behind it a little dove-cot. "Look a Poussin." It was the first time it had occurred to me to look at landscape in terms of art.[14]

The incident reveals Hemingway's affinity for Berenson. Hemingway's pronouncements on his ability to "make" a scene in the manner of Cezanne are now well known. Both men shared a great admiration for landscape painting and especially for Paul Cezanne.

Hemingway and Berenson never managed a genuine *rompre* although they did compare notes on many places, people, attitudes, and manners, and during their correspondence they revealed many of their mutual insecurities. They never met. Several times they were very close, and Berenson pleaded repeatedly for a visit from the Hemingways. He was aware that he had a short time to live, and since he had already enjoyed the company of Mary, he was anxious to see her again. "Caress Mary for me" was one of his warmest requests as he signed his BB to a letter which addressed Hemingway in "full Jovian splendor."[15]

Perhaps the closest the two friends ever came to a genuine *rompre* occurred when the Hemingways planned a visit to Florence while they were staying in Venice on their way back to Cuba after the disastrous African safari in 1954. The 89-year-old Berenson had many reservations about meeting Hemingway in person. as revealed by his diary entry for March 25, 1954:

> Ernest Hemingway is impending, and I look forward with a certain dread to seeing and knowing him in the flesh. Hitherto we have only corresponded. His letters seemed written when he was not quite sober, rambling and affectionate. I fear he may turn out too

animal, too overwhelmingly masculine, too Bohemian. He may expect me to drink and guzzle with him, and write me down as a muff. I know him only through his writing, which I admire greatly here and again, but seldom a whole book. What can he know of the real me? Has he seriously read anything I have written? Has he been taken by the myth? Has his present wife, whom I led through my garden some years ago, given him ideas about me? What, I wonder, does he expect? I dread arranged meetings, I prefer to meet people unexpectedly, casually, with no responsible feeling that I must see them again, or encounter resentment.

The following day, March 26, 1954, Berenson wrote Hemingway in Venice, .welcomed him back to Italy, and insisted that he looked "forward with keen zeal to seeing [him] in the flesh." As the letter continued, however, Berenson lamented the crowded calendar that always plagued him in the summer. So many visitors expected to stay for a meal. They would, however, be able to go for a long walk, but unfortunately there was no room for them to stay at "*I tatti*". Berenson concluded: "I mention this dolesome fact which will prevent my seeing you both *alone* as much as I should wish.[16] Hemingway took the letter as a rebuke. He used a long catalogue of his injuries suffered in the two air crashes as an excuse for putting off the trip to Florence, but he was obviously offended by Berenson's reluctance to see them alone. They would come down, he replied, some time when so many of his admirers were not around. The letter from Berenson had clearly offended Hemingway, and they never managed to regain their former intimacy. Berenson's lack of compassion and understanding for his injured friend, whose obituary had been flashed around the world after the two air crashes, was no doubt caused by the self-doubt and recrimination which Berenson suffered throughout most of his later life. The deterioration of Hemingway's mind and composure was evident in the frayed handwriting of the first letter he wrote to Berenson nine days after the crash.[17]The letter also included a grizzly photograph of Hemingway's badly burned left hand. Still apparently disappointed that they had not met, Berenson reminded Hemingway at Christmas in 1954: "Don't forget you are mortal"[18]

More important for the correspondence than this failure to meet at a very difficult time in Hemingway's life was the intimacy and cordiality which both men instinctively felt for each other. Carlos Baker included 13 of Hemingway's letters in his collection, and in his biography he makes a number of references to Hemingway's letters to Berenson, but essentially he used them to document Hemingway's location on certain dates. He makes no references to Berenson's letters to Hemingway. His statement that Hemingway "elbowed his way into the correspondence"[19] completely ignores the mutual sincerity, compassion, and admiration that dominates the communications of these two famous men. Completely lacking in Baker's references to the eight-year correspondence are the expressions of humor, warmth, encouragement, language, and learning which dominated their exchanges. Baker's "macho" image of Hemingway left little room for sophisticated conversation with a man like Berenson or compassion for Hemingway's earlier loss of his real father by suicide.

Hemingway wrote to Berenson for the same reason that he wrote to Malcolm Cowley and Arthur Mizener: he was lonely and bored in Cuba. But the personal dimension that reaches beyond these other exchanges is what makes this correspondence so significant. Hemingway constantly asks Berenson to write and let him know that he is well. His tenderness to Berenson as when he details his love for Mary[20] was frequently echoed in his honest concern for the old man's health and even his love of the Italian landscape. For example, he asked Berenson to "Remember [him] to any big slow oxen and to all cypress trees, all bends in the road, and to any hill you meet." There is never any question that they were addressing each other in the familiar "*tu*," but on one occasion Hemingway defined his understanding of their linguistic intimacy: "you alone, you only, you who I love, you who I see again, you with who I share a tribal secret."[21] .

Hemingway's intimacy was also flavored with a delicate humor. Writing about his son, Patrick, for example, and some of the difficulties of parenthood, he wrote to this world authority on Italian Renaissance art that Patrick was "sort of an angel; not Botticelli angel" but "Northern Cheyenne Indian angel where they have very good angels too." On another occasion while praising the natural beauty of Cuba, Hemingway wrote in the same tone:

> Lately we have had the curious juxtaposition of Venus, Jupiter. Mars and Mercury in the sky. I have never seen Venus so wonderful in my life and no one will again for a long time. Then. now. all the migratory birds are coming through and there are ten pairs of mocking birds nested here on the place. I play Bach on the phonograph to one and he learned it very well.[22]

When Berenson, with wobbly fingers, asked Hemingway to pray for him, Hemingway replied that he had already taken care of that. Not only had "a non-believing Northern Cheyenne ... pray[ed] for a Jew," in Chartres, Burgos, Segovia, and two minor places, but he apologized for not having prayed yet at "the home office, Santiago de Compostella" [23]. Later Hemingway admitted that he prayed for Berenson whenever he was in trouble[24] He had signed off a letter to Berenson with the reflection:

> I prayed for you all the time on the [African safari] whenever I would wake up in the night. I doubt whether it has any practical value but it is pleasant and healthy to do. I quit praying for myself in Spain in the war because it seemed too egotistical with everyone having it so bad. But now I pray for you, for Mary, for my grand-daughter. You were probably joking when you said to pray for you. But I don't think it could do any harm. The prayers of sinners, I believe, are especially potent.[25]

The subject of death and what would happen to them in the next world was a constant undercurrent of the correspondence. After Berenson had reminded Hemingway, "Don't forget that you are mortal,"[26] Hemingway advised Berenson that when he died he was not to tell Dante, if he saw him of their little joke about expecting to meet in an afterlife.[27] "Pity the poor people who believe in any other life," Hemingway, labeling himself as *El Profundo*, had written to Berenson a few months earlier. "If they really had any such dirty trick we will be together and have a fine time. You classify and I will make a running comment and we'll disturb the circles. Poor Dante. Maybe we can find him a job as concierge."[28] The witty and tender tones of the letters to Berenson were another of Hemingway's secrets and characterized none of his other sustained correspondence with the possible exception of the letters to his children. The tenderness suggests again that Hemingway was seeking not only the approval, but also the affection of a father.

The joke of the sinner sending secret letters to the saint was expanded in their continued discussion of the Hemingway he-man image as compared to the esthete. Berenson returned to the contrast time and again. It probably was the reason that they never met. Berenson focused constantly on the public image of Hemingway and seemed not to recognize the lonely man behind the hard-drinking, hard-whoring, and hard-fighting sporting man, apparently without recognizing the tenderness and compassion in his correspondent's letters. Perhaps, he mused to Hemingway, he himself had never lived. He wondered if Hemingway would put him down as a "muff." Berenson seemed to question the worth of his entire life in his letters to Hemingway.[29] He seemed especially depressed in the light of Hemingway's image. He had rarely played "the beast with two backs" but had to admit that compared to Santayana, he had led an adventurous and colorful life[30]

Santayana paid frequent visits to their exchanges. Santayana, also an immigrant Jew, had arrived in America from Avila. Spain. Berenson had originally immigrated with his family to the United States from Lithuania. Santayana, however. had preceded Berenson to Harvard by one year, and as a result Berenson always seemed on the defensive about Santayana, although in other contexts, when Harvard was not being considered, he would joke about him. Berenson felt that Santayana wrote beautifully and occasionally there was a good thought.[31] He had to admit, however, that the chief reason he wrote beautifully was that "he had never lived."[32] Hemingway was evidently reading Santayana at the time(there were five volumes by Santayana in Hemingway's library) and he was less compassionate than Berenson. In addition to dismissing Santayana as "a chickenshit philosopher" who died unloving and unloved, "except by nuns."[33] On one occasion he reflected at some length:

> If there is any point that I would try to make it is that if you come from Avila there is no mystery about Avila. I never knew Saint Teresa because she was before my time. If we had been contemporaries, I am quite sure we would have been good friends. The same with Juan de la Cruz. Quevedo I feel I know better than my brother. Santayana to me is a different business. Because he comes from a walled town he thinks that makes a difference. It makes no difference in the heart. Anyone who has lived in a walled town knows how much human shit there is on the ramparts and under the towers. We know who fought for it and helped build it and who did not. ... You know that what ruined, and what made Spain, was the Inquisition. They missed Santayana's family and he became a beautifully writing apologist for it. This is very unjust but you be patient with me too.[34]

Berenson constantly asked Hemingway to be patient with his almost illegible handwriting. The day before, however, Hemingway had promised that if Berenson insisted, he would try to envy Santayana as a "spiritual exercise."

This sort of talk, however. always brought on bouts of self-doubt for Berenson when he was confronted by the public image of Hemingway. This European dandy, brother-in-law of Bertrand Russell and all of the free-thinking that went with that circle, who openly lived for many years with a mistress married to another man, and associated with Oscar Wilde, confided his deepest sexual doubts and fears to Hemingway:

> What is life? Is it exercising to the utmost all ... one's animal functions? That seems to be what the likes of you seem to write about, do write about and picture that it is LIFE. Then poor ME has not lived at all. I have loved much, but fucked little (although ex-

quisitely and ecstatically as you sip a priceless liqueur. I have never been drunk and do not like a drink except of wines too expensive for my pocket. I never fought nor bled. In short I have never been a he man. Would you write me down as a muff? Not if you knew me I hope. And bluff. Don Emesto. Where is man to be?[35]

Hemingway's reply to this self-doubt was a compassionate and very different reply than might be expected from the public image of Hemingway which Berenson had insisted on addressing:

Please don't get mixed up about LIFE. That is only a picture magazine. I always joke and much of it is gallows humor. You must truly know that no matter how stupid people act, in order not to argue with fools. Any writer that you respect at all, or that has given you pleasure, can think a little bit.[36]

Later, Hemingway wrote that Berenson should consider him as his "pup" because Hemingway had been educated by his "god-damned beautifully worked out lovely books."[37] Berenson was amazed that the famous writer would denigrate himself to an art historian. In his own insecurities, Berenson seemed incapable of recognizing Hemingway's longing for an authoritative father.

Hemingway appreciated the beauty in Berenson's books but admitted, "I cannot write beautifully but I can write with great accuracy (sometimes; I hope) and the accuracy makes a sort of beauty."[38] "You lave done a good job," he wrote encouragingly to Berenson, "and left things in order."[39] Hemingway especially envied Berenson's managed and ordered library. Since his own had been looted and pilfered,[40] he felt Berenson was better off: "You are always letter off than me because you have more books. Thank God for books."[41]

Writing and reading in fact made up a good portion of their correspondence. Hemingway warmed to the subject as he wrote to the learned art critic. His language bridged the gap between writing and painting. Whether Hemingway sensed Berenson's antipathy to more recent art is not always clear. Berenson claimed to have lost interest in painting after Matisse."[42] Little was written, however, about specific painters, but Hemingway took pains to define his writing in visual terms. He could "make country" he wrote on two occasions,[43] but that this was very difficult. Another time, he admitted that he could "make" people because he had "a perfect ear."[44] He felt an "obligation," he insisted, to write fiction, however, because that was the way that he could "'invent" in such a way that he would create fiction that was "truer than things can be true."[45] As he had written to Malcolm Cowley on a number of occasions, Hemingway repeated to Berenson that fiction writers were only liars who steal from others. What they don't steal they invent.[46] . And he returned to the lying metaphor several times not only to analyze his own methods, but also to bolster the elder writer's genre of writing as he denigrates his own:

> Writers of fiction are only super-liars who if they know enough and are disciplined can make their lies truer than the truth. If you have fought and diced and served at court and gone to the wars and know navigation, sea-manship, the bad world and the great world and the different countries and other things then you have good knowledge to lie out of. That is all a writer of fiction is.[47]

Berenson had been complaining about how difficult it was to get started on a new book that he had been planning for some time although he wondered if his work was not all a terrible waste of time. Hemingway continues with, "don't write silly stuff about wasting your life. It was in doing what you had to do that you learned what it is worth while to say now .... You [should] start to write the book now." Hemingway had had his own problems when he started writing as he frankly wrote to Berenson:

> I had found the paragraph almost impossible. The chapter, I knew was beyond me. And the writing of a whole novel seemed like an assault on the Himalayas. But I knew I had to do it so I wrote one. When I wrote as a kid it seemed so easy but when I had started try-ing to make country that you could walk back into

and to learn what it was in speech that your ear actually retained and to try to move people emotionally with the landscape without being descriptive then writing got harder and harder to do. It still is damned hard and it is only the un-avaidable [sic] awkwardnesses that show. Peple [sic] think that is your style. And other poor bastards copy the awkwardnesses and think that is the secret.[48]

The dialogue on writing had started over Berenson's admiration for *The Old Man and the Sea*. Berenson admired Hemingway because he felt that he wrote from "within" about "the creative spasm"[49] while he, of course, only dealt with the end product. Berenson had endeared himself to Hemingway early in their correspondence by comparing the style of *The Old Man and the Sea* to that of Homer and by saying that he much preferred Hemingway's old fisherman to Herman Melville's Ahab.[50] Hemingway responded by writing that Moby-Dick was good "journalism" which resulted only in a "forced rhetorical epic."[51] He compliments "the only critic I respect" and then pays tribute to the knowledge which is behind *The Old Man and the Sea* and which the great connoisseur should appreciate:

> There isn't any symbolism (mis-spelled). The sea is the sea. The old man is an old man. The boy is a boy and the fish is a fish. The sharks are all sharks-no better and no worse. All the symbolism that people say is shit. What goes beyond is what you see beyond when you know. A writer should know too much.[52]

The thought, if not the diction, seems borrowed from Henry James's "The Art of Fiction." If Berenson recognized the language of his old friend from Cambridge with whom he had spent many hours, he did not report it to Hemingway.

Hemingway was so delighted with his correspondent's praise, however, that he could not resist asking him for a blurb to be printed on the book jacket. After Hemingway sent the galleys to him, Berenson sent the following statement to the London publishers of *The Old Man and the Sea*:

> Hemingway's Old Man and the Sea is an idyll
> of the sea as sea, as un-Byronic and un-Melvillian
> as Homer himself and communicated in a prose as
> calm and compelling as Homer's verse. No real art-
> ist symbolizes or allegorizes-and Hemingway is a
> real artist—but every real work of art exhales sym-
> bols and allegories. So does this short but not small
> masterpiece. Bernard Berenson.[53]

Hemingway probably felt that a testimonial from someone with Berenson's stature could be used to hold off the critics and Hemingway bashers who had sneered at *Across the River and into the Trees*. *The Old Man and the Sea*, however, needed no help from Berenson. His comment, nevertheless, did appear in Scribner's advertisement for *The Old Man and the Sea*, above similar accolades from Cyril Connolly, Malcolm Cowley, Carlos Baker, and Somerset Maugham.[54] In appreciation, Hemingway sent a highly annotated copy of the ad to Berenson with a notation at the top: "File under: Where Do We Go From Here? EH."

Hemingway also wrote Berenson many anecdotes about writing *The Sun Also Rises* and *A Farewell to Arms*. Hemingway wrote to him as a worldly-wise sage and reassured Berenson that no writer really reveals himself in writing. Berenson was nevertheless filled with self-doubt, not only about his writing but about the entire meaning of his life. He saw the life of the connoisseur, especially as revealed in his writings, as one of waste. Just as Berenson insisted on constantly addressing the public image of Hemingway, so Hemingway constantly addressed the public image of Berenson. Neither seemed to recognize or at least admit that they were writing to someone who in his private life was more insecure and troubled than the public image which was manufactured. Perhaps they recognized the dichotomy, and in spite of much frankness, each respected the loneliness and privacy of the other. Their affection for each other was constantly apparent and may have been augmented by this mutual recognition. In a rare burst of affection Hemingway admitted that Berenson was one of his heroes.

As the two correspondents grew closer together, they exchanged impressions and prejudices not only about Santayana, as already mentioned, but about many figures who reveal the breadth and depth of their common interest. Among them: Koestler; Malraux, a liar (Hemingway's contempt began during the Spanish Civil War; Berenson liked and admired him); D. H. Lawrence; Gertrude and Leo Stein (Gertrude hated Berenson); Joyce; Thomas Wolfe; Lillian Ross ("like being good friends with a circular saw"); Sherwood Anderson (Hemingway did not trust "anyone with a Southern accent"); Dante; Henry James ("I was wounded badly before Henry James received O.M. for his patriotic sentiments"); Unamuno; Thomas Mann (Hemingway liked *Buddenbrooks*); Pound who wrote "U.T." [Unknown Tongue]; Faulkner ("When I get tired sometimes I imitate Faulkner a little bit just to show him how it should be done. It is like loosening up with a five finger exercise"); Joan Miró; Mary McCarthy; Rosamund Lehman; and El Greco. This listing is by no means complete, but simply suggestive of the content, tone, and direction of their rich and revealing exchanges.

One is constantly wondering how much Hemingway knew about Berenson. Did he know that Berenson was an intimate of Henry James as a student at Harvard and later a good friend of his brother, William? Did he know that Berenson's wife/mistress, Mary Costello, was a good friend of Whitman? These puzzles increase as the correspondence continues and. intensify the unfortunate fact that the two men never met.

One of the aspects of Hemingway that intrigued Berenson most was Hemingway's legendary success with women. As a product of that liberal British circle that included Oscar Wilde and Bertrand Russell, Berenson was constantly asking for details about the sexual exploits of many of the visitors who sought him out at "*I Tatti*." It was Mary's visit there in 1948 that had started the correspondence in the first place, and Berenson was always looking for juicy details. Sexual innuendo was frequently just beneath the surface of their communications and often surfaced. Mary Hemingway recalled how in their first and only meeting Berenson had startled her. She had been sent into the garden to tell him tea was served:

"What number are you" asked Mr. B.
"Sir? Do you number your guests?"

"Wife," said he, excusing my density, and when I told him "number four" he asked how it was Ernest had managed to get through so many wives.

"I have no simple answer for that. sir," said I as we moved up toward the house.

"Of course, Ernest is a man of tremendous energy and exuberance."

"Does he demonstrate those characteristics in bed?" the renowned art expert asked in the most casual tones, totally flummoxing me. I was relieved to turn him over to the other guests and Lucy [Moorehead], noticing my strawberry-red face, giggled knowingly.[55]

In a similar vein, Berenson's biographer. Meryle Secrest. records a meeting between Martha Gellhorn, Hemingway's third wife, and the aging, but still amorous Berenson:

He used to stay in a hotel in Rome to which I'd be invited for dinner; there were practically pink-shaded lamps," Martha Gellhorn remembers. "I am an exceedingly unswoony lady, and at a given moment, he'd sit next to me on the sofa and I'd say, 'Nothing doing. Keep your little hands to yourself.' [56]

When Berenson was almost 90, he asked Hemingway to caress Mary for him[57] and wrote that Hemingway's description of a German/Indonesian houseguest [probably Herta Klausser][58] "warmed his cold balls."[59] Undoubtedly, a father/son relationship was not the only explanation for the two correspondents' interest in each other.

Because of Berenson's long association with Martha Gellhorn, it was not long before Hemingway was asked "when in genial mood, all passion spent" to write Berenson about his third wife.[60] Hemingway responded immediately but didn't send the letter until about a month later when he was in France. Basically Hemingway is kind and gentle towards Martha, a woman over whom he had spent a great amount of spirit in a waste of shame, but his comments reveal that there was a great deal of bitterness remaining between them. Martha's correspondence to Berenson makes it quite clear that after they had separated. she was terrified of accidentally bumping into Hemingway. Whether she would meet Berenson at the Hotel *Europa* would depend on "how Ernest-free the Venetian waterways" were.[61] Not always overly generous, Hemingway resorted to Spanish slang for his former wife: "Miss Martha was a *conejo* and I was well deceived."[62]

Hemingway appears to have been most terrified, however, of her ambition. It led to innumerable arguments and jealousies that he was later amused by, but that obviously left them incompatible. Hemingway had mixed feelings about writing to Berenson about his third wife. He knew that honesty would be difficult and he also felt she had made a fool out of him and so the problem was truly complicated:

> B.B. you asked me to write you about Miss Mar-
> tha. So I started dutifully and had a wonderful time
> writing what you should never write. But then I real-
> ized that no one, no matter how truthful they think
> they are writing. can write truthfully in the round
> about a personal thing. Also having lived much of my
> life in France. Italy. Spain and here [Cuba] I have the
> Latin's hatred of being a fool and the Latin contempt
> for a fool. When the fool was yourself the contempt
> increases.[63]

Hemingway's analysis of Martha for Berenson tells as much about him as it does about Martha. His recollections also tell us a great deal about his theories about the relationship between fact and fiction. If he had trouble remembering many of the details, how could a biographer capture the reality? His reminiscences of Martha read much like his letters to Mizener about Fitzgerald; Hemingway is the real topic. Hemingway admitted to Berenson that he was frightened of ambitious women, and as a result he avoided them. Martha's ambition troubled him, and so he recognized that although he was in love with her, he didn't really like her very much. In spite of his reservations, he recognized her generosity and devotion to a cause. The causes she espoused were not always the highest in

Hemingway's ranking. For example, he wrote to Berenson that even though she read and spoke French very well, the only French books she ever read were by Colette. The only reason that she read them was because Colette had been the mistress of Henri du Juvenal, and since she had been the mistress of young Bertrand de Juvenal, her reasons for indulging in such reading were questionable. The differences in their tastes in reading had been a considerable source of difficulty. Hemingway admitted that as a reader he corrupted easily, and as a result he picked up Martha's passion for detective fiction which became their substitute for thinking. Not only did she not love good books, but she did not care about pictures or good music. Little wonder that this admirer of Cezanne and Bach, among many other mentors, found himself married to a woman whom he loved but didn't like.

Probably the strangest difference between them was their different attitude toward war. Hemingway's contempt for her beautiful uniforms and tailored dresses that would show up even the highest generals in a war zone was scathing. He thought that she had never seen a man killed in battle, and as a result, she not only loved war and all of its trappings, its glamour and the attention a beautiful girl receives when she moves around 2 million men who have left their women behind, but she also loved the money she made from the whole nasty business of war: "she probably made more tax-free money writing about our dead and about atrocities than any female author made since Harriet Beecher Stowe wrote Uncle Tom's Cabin."[64] She was also capable of making him feel like a "damned fool and a shit" for leaving his wife and children. He used alcohol as an anesthetic and sunk so low, he repeated to Berenson, that he even read detective stories.

Hemingway went on to a more generous assessment of their relationship, especially commenting on Martha's graciousness toward his children, but the entire tone of the long letter[65] which no doubt titillated Berenson, reveals the chasm between Hemingway and his third wife which was filled with enmity, bitterness and despair.

A typical confrontation, for example, occurred during the invasion of Normandy. Hemingway was flown over to France by the RAF, but Martha had to go by boat.[66] She was not amused. Martha had insisted, he continued, that he pack two pin-stripe suits, a blue serge suit and several tweed jackets, an approach to haberdashery that evidently clouded or began many of their bitter quarrels. Hemingway had asked her if they were going on an invasion or to "some ball room banana festival." But he took the clothes "to be a good boy." Not only were his clothes in need of improvement, but she tried to rid him of his middle-westem accent so that he would fit in better with the social set in England where Hemingway always felt out of place. He also admitted to Berenson that "after Martha" he frequently used the reading of detective fiction as a substitute for thinking.[67] His library indeed still has vast amounts of the genre and his son Patrick told me that his father returned from World War II carrying everything ever written by Georges Simenon.

Hemingway was quick to admit that although he found Martha difficult, he was also bad for her.[68] Berenson assured Hemingway that Martha always spoke well of him both as a worker and as a novelist. He omits what she said about him as a man. After Hemingway's rather frank letter, Berenson assured him that he had seen Martha only once in two or three years[69] and, of course, never admitted to his meeting her at a hotel at any time.

Hemingway's reputation and rather free talk about loose women struck a sympathetic and responsive chord in Berenson. Martha's ghosts were well gone by the time Hemingway visited the Hotel Floridita in Madrid with his fourth wife, but Hemingway returned again and again to the subject of Martha during his correspondence with Berenson. By 1956 he was both horrified and relieved that his third marriage had not ended more disastrously than it did. The words of Martha still plagued his reminiscences: "We were giants and could have had the world at our feet." To which Hemingway could only add: "Good God! Perhaps it would be best if Mary McCarthy, Malraux and Martha were all hanged—upside down."[70]

Berenson's letters were filled with the recognition that he had a short time to live. Gradually the same feeling overtook Hemingway as he admitted in 1957 that he had seen "many people [that] year [who] made it easier to think of leaving this world than [he] believed it would ever be."[71] In fact. he wrote at one time earlier, that dying was "simpler than going to the bathroom."[72] The two writers shared a diminishing view of the world, and in all of their sexual banter recalling of old times and reminiscences about comfortable and meaningful artists and landscapes, they both recognized that the world they once loved was now used up and mutilated. In spite of Hemingway's filial gesture to Berenson that he was writing to "divert [him] with funny letters" the ultimate tone of their correspondence was captured in one of Hemingway's reminiscences:

> Maybe because you have complicated blood. as
> I have, you would understand this. One time when I
> was out at the Wind River reservation a very old In-
> dian spoke to me and said, "You Indian Boy?" I said,
> "Sure." He said. "Cheyenne?" I said. "Sure." He said,
> "Long time ago good. Now no good."[73]

A good measure of what Hemingway wrote to Berenson has been noted before. What is especially significant in addition to the fact that Hemingway counted among his close friends one of the world's greatest art critics is the tone of wit, humor. compassion, delight, and honest affection that dominated this eight-year correspondence. More and more the intimate glimpse of Hemingway in the turtleneck sweater captured by Joseph Karsh, who said that he never met a person more insecure than Ernest Hemingway, is replacing the rather macho personality created by Maxwell Perkins and Carlos Baker and perpetuated by many others.

It is unfortunate that all of the correspondence (see Appendix II) was not included in Carlos Baker's edition of Hemingway's letters. Even then, however, Berenson's contribution would be lacking. Since Berenson's letters are rapidly deteriorating because of the poor quality of the paper on which they were written, and in spite of the fact that they are carefully preserved in the John F. Kennedy Library in Boston, the extent of this rare expression of mutual love and admiration will probably never be completely known. Those letters by Hemingway not included in Baker's edition of the letters are virtually inaccessible at Villa "*I Tatti*." I understand that current efforts are being made to include these letters in the new edition of Hemingway's letters. This brief overview of the content has been an attempt to record one of Hemingway's most intimate relationships during the final years of his life. Many harsh notes have been uttered about this troubled time of his life, but the difficulties and loneliness of those final years in Cuba were perhaps best recorded in Hemingway's rambling letters to Bernard Berenson. The portrait of Hemingway staring at that blank white wall in front of his typewriter or at the gathering smog over his beloved Havana is best captured by Berenson's recent biographer, Meryle Secrest:

> If Hemingway's letters are ever published. they will demonstrate that the legend of Hemingway does an injustice to the reality of the man. His letters to Berenson are a delight, full of wit. anecdote, and imaginative invention. They are rambling and discursive, with much parenthetical exclamation and explanation. and are, in fact, so spontaneous that they will banish forever the image of Hemingway as an anguished writer painfully producing a sentence every third day. They are indomitable and life-enhancing letters. full of whimsical reminiscence and unguarded insights into himself, written in a labored hand, like a child learning to write. They show a wistful. tender, and loving man. transparently insecure, and one diametrically opposite to the almost ludicrous ultramasculine image offered to the world.[74]

The problems of their public images dominated the correspondence and caused a constant tension and separation in their communication, but Berenson's delight in their exchange was no less positive than Hemingway's love of the connoisseur from "*I Tatti*" who signed one of his last letters with the telling recognition of a proud father: "My best to Mary and your magnificent self."[75]

Afterword

Mary Hemingway told me on one of our productive visits to her apartment in New York City that she had on two occasions prepared detailed opportunities with permissions for her and Carlos Baker to visit Cuba and interview a wide spectrum of Cubans who knew Hemingway. For no reason and at the last moment Baker cancelled both trips. My personal impression based on the tone of her conversation and the record of Dr Herrera provided by Nabokov is that Baker had great trepedations concerning Hemingway's relation to the Cuban revolution and Fidel Castro. The board of Princeton University which had the ominous ear of Charles Scribner. Jr no doubt feared that a sympathetic view of Hemingway's obvious sympathy with the Cuban revolution would reflect negatively on the involvement of Princeton in Cuba and the United States official embargo. With the August 12, 2009 Latin American Herald Tribune reporting that the US government forced Hemingway to leave Cuba or he would be considered a traitor and McCleans reporting that a play based on Hemingway's final days has been mercifully closed, the story of Hemingway's twenty years in Cuba is continuing to unfold. The United States embargo and resulting isolationism has dealt a great blow to Hemingway scholarship. Hemingway's honest self-appraisal of his method and technique has been lost. Since many of Hemingway's closest friends have passed away the truth is more difficult to uncover. I sincerely hope that resurrecting Dr Herrera's insights from Russian obscurity, Malcolm Cowley's insightful impressions hidden in puzzling obscurity and Bernard Berenson's insights obscured in a restricted library will add to the accumulation of attempts to analyze Hemingway's incontrovertable   affect on fictional techniques far beyond his obvious contribution to English fiction. His Cuban years may eventually prove to be more critically insightful than all the Latin wandering in Europe.

Appendix I

Log of Ernest Hemingway/Malcolm Cowley Correspondence

DATE	LETTER	LOCATION *
June 9, 1937	MC to EH	KL
_____, 1940	EH to MC	unknown
Sep 3,1945	EH to MC	unknown
Oct 17, 1945	EH to MC	KL, Baker
Oct 28, 1947,	MC to EH	unknown
Nov 14, 1947	EH to MC	unknown
Jan 15, 1948	EH to MC	unknown
Apr 9, 1948	EH to MC	unknown
Apr 13, 1948	EH to MC	unknown
May 25, 1948	MC to EH	unknown
Jun 9, 1948	EH to MC	unknown
Jun 22, 1948	MC to EH	unknown
Jun 25, 1948	EH to MC	unknown
Jun 29, 1948	EH to MC	unknown
Jul 5, 1948	EH to MC	unknown
Jul 11, 1948	MC to EH	KL
Jul 15, 1948	EH to MC	unknown
Aug 5 1948	MC to EH	unknown
Aug 19, 1948	EH to Mc	unknown
Aug 25, 1948	EH to MC	unknown
Aug 28, 1948	MC to EH	not preserved
Sept 5, 1946	EH to MC	unknown
Nov 8, 1948	MC to EH	unknown

Nov 16, 1948	EH to MC	unknown
Nov 29, 1948	EH to MC	unknown
Dec 3, 1948	EH to DeVoto	unknown
Jan 1,1949	MC to EH	unknown
Jan 24, 1949	EH to MC	unknown
Feb 9, 1949	EH to MC	unknown
Feb 9, 1949	M to MC	unknown
Feb 10, 1949	EH to MC	unknown
Feb 17, 1949	MC to M	unknown
Mar 8, 1949	EH to MC	unknown
May 3, 1949	MC to EH	KL
Jun 10 1049	EH to MC	unknown
Sep 24, 1949	MC to EH	unknown
Sep 29, 1949	EH to MC	unknown
Oct 7, 1949	MC to EH	KL
Oct 11, 1949	EH to MC	Baker
Dec 14, 1949	MC to EH	unknown
Jan 27, 1950	EH to MC	unknown
Apr 18m 1951	MC to EH	KL
Apr 19, 1951	EH to MC	unknown
May 9, 1951	MC to EH	KL
May 13, 1951	EH to MC	unknown
May 19, 1951	MC to EH	KL
Jun 1, 1951	EH to MC	unknown
Jun 2, 1951	EH to MC	unknown
Jun 8, 1951	MC to EH	unknown
Jun 15, 1951	EH to MC	unknown
Jul 19, 1951	MC to EH	KL
Jul 24, 1951	EH to MC	unknown
Aug 11, 1951	MC to EH	KL (includes copy of Cowley's introduction to the Portable Fitzgerald)
Sep 16, 1951	EH to MC	unknown
Nov 3, 1951	MC to EH	KL (includes information on copyright law)
Nov 8, 1951	EH to MC	unknown
Nov 14, 1951	MC to EH	KL
Nov 20, 1951	EH to MC	unknown

Dec 14, 1951	EH to MC	unknown
Dec 25, 1951	MC to EH	KL
Dec 31, 1951	EH to MC	unknown
Jan 17, 1952	EH to MC	unknown
Jan 28, 1952	MC to EH	KL
____,1952	EH to MC	unknown
May 4, 1952	EH to MC	unknown
May 16, 1952	EH to MC	unknown
May 24, 1952	MC to EH	KL
May 29, 1952	EH to MC	unknown
Aug 3, 1952	MC to EH	unknown
Aug, 1952	EH to MC	unknown
Dec, 1952	EH to MC	unknown

*Key:

KL = Hemingway Collection, John F. Kennedy Library, Colombia Point, Boston, Mass.

M = Mary Welsh Hemingway

Baker = Carlos Baker. *Earnest Hemingway: Selected Letters, 1917-1961*. New York: Charles Scribner's Sons. 1981.

Unknown = Read by me in home of gracious owners, Marsha and Maurice Neville, but sold at auction in 2004. Anonymous owner has prohibited access nor identified location. (Selby Kiffer to JDB, July 8, 2009)

Appendix II

Log of the Ernest Hemingway/Bernard Berenson Correspondence

DATE	LETTER	DATELINE	PRESENT LOCATION
25 Aug 49	EH (M) to BB	FV, Cuba	I Tatti;; Baker, 666.
14 Nov 49	MH to BB	FV, Cuba	I Tatti
26 Dec 50	BB to EH	Settignano	KL
31 Dec 50	EH to BB	FV, Cuba	I Tatti
6 Sept 52	BB to EH	Vallombrosa/ Settignano	KL
13 Sept 52	EH (M) to BB	FV, Cuba	I Tatti, Baker, 780
21 Sept 52	BB to EH	Vallombrosa/ Settignano	KL
27 Sept 52	Cable: BB to Belleville	Vallambrosa	KL
2 Oct 52 (Included several newspaper clippings and reviews)	EH to BB	FV, Cuba	I Tatti, Baker, 784
10 Oct 52	BB to Eh	Settignano	KL

Date	Direction	Place	Source
14 Oct 52 (included newspaper clippings)	EH to BB	FV, Cuba	I Tatti, Baker, 788
11 Nov 52	BB to EH	Rome	KL
25 Nov 52	BB to EH	Rome	KL
4 Dec 52	BB to EH		?
24 Jan 53	EH to BB	FV, Cuba	I Tatti, Baker, 801
12 Feb 53	BB to EH		?
17 Feb 53	EH to BB	FV, Cuba	I Tatti, Baker, 803
28 Feb 53	BB to EH	Settignano	KL
6 Mar 53	EH to BB	FV, Cubba	I Tatti
15 Mar 53	BB to EH	Settignano	KL
20-22 Mar 53	EH to BB	FV, Cuba	I Tatti, Baker, 808
29 Mar 53	BB to EH	?	KL
13 Apr 53	EH to BB	FV, Cuba	I Tatti
22 Apr 53	BB to EH	Settignano	KL
4 May 53	EH to BB	Ruar del Rio, Cuba	I Tatti
21 May 53	BB to EH	Messanio	KL
27 May 53 (sent 10 Jun 53	EH to BB	FV, Cuba	I Tatti
10 Jun 53	EH to BB	FV, Cuba	I Tatti
22 Jun 53	BB to EH	Naples	KL
11 Aug 53	EH to BB	at sea	I Tatti, Baker, 823
15 Sep 53	EH to BB	Kenya/ Tanganika border	I Tatti, Baker, 825
29 Sep 53	BB to EH	Masera	KL
31 Sep 53	BB to EH	?	KL
15 Nov 53	EH to BB	Kenya	I Tatti
22 Nov 53	BB to EH	Rome	KL
23 Jan 54	Cable: BB to EH	?	?
2 Feb 54	EH to BB	Kenya	I Tatti, Baker, 827
26 Mar 54	BB to EH	Settignano	KL
29 Mar 54	EH to BB	Venice	I Tatti
3 April 54	BB to EH	Settignano	KL
4 Apr 54	EH to BB	Venice	I Tatti
6 Apr 54	BB to EH	Settignano	KL
9 Apr 54 (sent 1 May 54	EH to BB	Venice	I Tatti

1 May 54	EH to BB	Venice	I Tatti
29 Aug 54	EH to BB	FV, Cuba	I Tatti
11 Sep 54	BB to EH	Vallambrosa	KL
4 Sep 54	EH tp BB	?	See BB, 17 Sep 54
17 Sep 54	BB to EH	Settignano	KL
24 Sep 55	EH to BB	FV, Cuba	I Tatti, Baker, 836
22 Dec 54	BB to EH	Settignano	KL
9 Jul 55 (sent 10 Apr 56)	EH to BB	Key West	I Tatti
18 Sep 55	EH to BB	FV, Cuba	I Tatti, Baker, 846
29 Sep 55	BB to EH	Venice	KL
4 Oct 55	EH to BB	FV, Cuba	I Tatti
19 Oct 55	BB to EH	Venice	KL
2 Nov 55	BB to EH	Settignano	KL
21 Dec 55	BB to EH	Settignano	KL
2 Mar 56	EH to BB	FV, Cuba	I Tatti
8 Aug 56	BB to EH	Settignano	KL
19 Aug 56	EH to BB	Paris	I Tatti
30 Apr 57	EH to BB	FV, Cuba	I Tatti
21 Aug 57	MH to BB	FV, Cuba	I Tatti
24 Aug 57	EH to BB	FV, Cuba	I Tatti

Key: FV, Cuba: Finca Vigia, San Francisco de Paula, Cuba.
I Tatti: via di Vincigliata 26, 50135, Florence, Italy
(M) post scripts by Mary Hemingway, none of which were included in Baker's Edition of the letters
KL: Hemingway's Collection, John F. Kennedy Library, Boston , MA

Appendix III

Books in Berenson's Library by or about Ernest Hemingway

Cowley, Malcolm, ed. *Hemingway*. The Viking Portable Library. New York: The Viking Press, 1944.

Eastman, Max. *Great Companions*. London: Museum Press Ltd., 1959. "The Great and Small Ernest Hemingway," pp. 32-58.

Hemingway, Ernest. *Across the River and into the Trees*. London: Jonathan Cape, 1950.

_____. *The Essential Hemingway*. London: Jonathan Cape, 1947.

_____. *A Farewell to Arms*. New York: Charles Scribner's Sons, 1929.

_____. *The Old Man and the Sea*. New York: Charles   Scribner's Sons, 1952.

(Card in envelope attached: "Dear Ber. B. Hope that you are well and this won't bore you. Mary sends her love. Maybe we'll all learn how to write some time. It shouldn't be difficult if there was time enough. Your friend and admirer, E. Hemingway. ")

_____.. *To Have and Have Not*. London: Jonathan Cape, 1937.

New Republic. 40th Anniversary Issue. 131:21. Nov. 22, 1954. "Italy-1927" by Ernest Hemingway.

Wilson, Edmund. *The Wound and the Bow*. Cambridge, Mass.: Houghton Mifflin Company, 1941. "Hemingway-Gauge of Morale," pp. 214-242.

Source: Library catalogue at "*I Tatti*"

Books in Hemingway's Library by or about Bernard Berenson:

Berenson, Bernard. *Aesthetics and History in the Visual Arts*. New York: Pantheon, 1948.

_____. *The Italian Painters of the Renaissance*. London: Oxford, 1948.

_____. *Italian Pictures of the Renaissance: A List of the Principal Artists and Their Works*. with an Index of Places. Oxford: Clarendon, 1932.

_____. *Rumor and Reflection*. New York: Simon Shuster & Sons, 1952

_____, *Seeing and Knowing*. New York: Macmillan, 1954.

_____. *Sketch for a Self-Portrait*. New York: Pantheon, 1949.

Ostyn-Owen. William. *Bibliografia di Bernard Berenson*. Milan: Electra, 1955.

Source: James D. Brasch and Joseph Sigman. *Hemingway's Library: A Composite Record* (New York: Garland Press. 1981).

End Notes

Notes for Chapter 1

[1]   See Mary Welsh Hemingway, *How It Was* (New York: Knopf, 1976), 504ff.

[2]   There have been a number of "travelogue" articles, which provide little in the way of detailed information. For example, Kenneth Tynan, "A Visit to Havana," *Holiday*, 27 (February 1960),50-58; Sally Belfrage, "Haunted House of Ernest Hemingway," *Esquire*, 59 (February 1963), 66-67; Robert Manning, "Hemingway in Cuba," *The Atlantic Monthly*, 216 (August 1965), 101-108.

[3]   Carlos Baker describes a scene which took place in 1959: "A crowd with banners had gathered at Havana airport to welcome him home. Reporters asked what he thought of the increasing American coldness toward Castro. He deplored it, saying that after twenty years' residence he considered himself a true Cuban. To prove it, he kissed the hem of a Cuban flag.": *Ernest Hemingway A Life Story*. New York: Scribners, 1969, p. 551.

[4]   Evidently, Castro said much the same thing to Hemingway. See Mary Hemingway, p. 484: "On the way home [from a meeting with Castro] in the car Ernest murmured, 'He said he'd read The Bell in Spanish and used its ideas in the Sierra Maestra.' " For another version of this indebtedness see Kenneth Tynan, "A Visit to Havana," *Holiday*, 27 (February 1960), p. 58.

[5]   See James McLendon, *Papa: Hemingway in Key West* (Miami: E. A. Seeman, 1972), pp. 127, 195.

[6]   See A. E. Hotchner, *Papa Hemingway: A Personal Memoir* (New York: Random House, 1966), p. 13.

7   Ernest Hemingway to Arthur Mizener, 1 June 1950. Robert Manning recalled hearing a mixed program of Scarlatti, Beethoven, Oscar Peterson, and Louis Armstrong one morning when he was a guest at the *Finca*. "Hemingway in Cuba," *The Atlantic Monthly*, 216 (August 1965), p. 104.

8   For reproductions of these paintings see Emily Stipes Watts, *Ernest Hemingway and the Arts.*Urbana: University of Illinois Press, 1971.

9   See Mary Hemingway, pp. 485, 505-508, for additional comments on the Hemingway paintings.

10   The only known record of the books in Hemingway's library is an inventory prepared by Cuban officials: *Catalogo de la Biblioteca del Museo Hemingway* (Havana, 1966). A microfilm copy of this catalogue was obtained apparently with some difficulty by a German scholar from the *Biblioteca Nacional Jose Marti* in Havana. See Hans-Joachim Kann, "Ernest Hemingway and the Arts-A Necessary Addendum," *Fitzgerald/Hemingway Annual 1974* (Englewood, Co!.: Microcard Editions Books, 1975), pp. 145-154. See especially fn. 3, p. 153. This inventory is a non-alphabetical shelf-list of 1076 pages. It is divided into nine volumes: *Torno I, Sala; Torno II, Biblioteca, Estantes 1-6; Torno III, Biblioteca, Estantes 7-12 y mesas; Torno IV, Cuarto Visita; Torno V, Cuarto Estudio; Torno VI, Dormitorio Hemingway; Torno VII, Dormitorio Sra. Hemingway; Torno VIII, La Casita; Torno IX, La Torre.*

11   Mary Hemingway to Brasch and Sigman (New York, 22 January 1977); taped conversation. Mrs. Hemingway also said that when she cleaned up the house she placed the books in any empty spaces she could find. Manning in 1965 described the books in the library (i.e. the room) as "carefully divided into history, military books, biography, geography, natural history, some fiction, and a large collection of maps," p. 103. We saw no evidence of such division.

12   "April 8, 1955 with Hemingway: Unedited Notes on a Visit to Finca Vigia," *Fitzgerald/Hemingway Annual 1970* (Washington, D.C.: NCR/ Microcard Editions, 1970), p. 110.

13   See Joseph Blotner, *William Faulkner's Library: A Catalogue.* Richmond: University Press of Virginia, 1964.

14   *Hemingway's First War: The Making of A Farewell to ;Arms* (Princeton, N.].: Princeton University Press, 1976). See also Robert O. Stephens, "Hemingway's Riddle of Kilimanjaro: Idea and Image," *American Literature*, 32 (March 1960), p. 84-87. Stephens describes Hemingway's dependence on Hans Meyer's *Across East African*

Glaciers (London: Philip, 1891); Mrs. Hemingway brought this volume with her when she left Cuba in 1961.

Notes for Chapter 2

1   Charles Scribner's Sons, New York, 1981.

2   Ernest Hemingway to Bernard Berenson, 24 Sept. 1954. *Ernest Hemingway: Selected Letters, 1917-1961*, ed. Carlos Baker. New York: Charles Scribner's Sons, 1981, p.837.

3   Ernest Hemingway, *A Moveable Feast*. New York: Charles Scribner's Sons, 1964. The quoted passage is from the preface, the authorship of which is unclear. The minor omissions, adjustments and alterations to the manuscript of *A Moveable Feast* are discussed by Gerry Brenner in "Are we Going to Hemingway's Feast?" *American Literature*, 54 # 4, Dec., 1982, pp. 528-544. See also Jacqueline Tavernier-Courbin, "The Mystery of the Ritz-Hotel Papers, *College Literature*, 7 (1980), pp.289-303 and "The Manuscripts of *A Moveable Feast*," *Hemingway Notes*, 6 (1981), pp.9-15.

4   Hemingway Collection, John F. Kennedy Library, Boston, Mass. ROLL 19, T 178, 3 pp. My emphasis. This copy is taken from the holograph text # 178 (179 is typewritten with no changes.)

5   I am endebted to Alfred Rice of the Hemingway Foundation for permission to publish this manuscript material.

6   Roll 19 # 187, John F. Kennedy Library.

7   "An Alpine Idyll", *The Short Stories of Ernest Hemingway*. New York: Charles Scribner's Sons, 1966, p. 345.

8   Ernest Hemingway, *A Moveable Feast*. New York: Charles Scribner's Sons, 1964, p. 156. My emphasis.

9   Lillian Ross, "How Do You Like It Now, Gentlemen?", which is most easily available in Hemingway: *A Collection of Critical Essays*. ed. Robert P. Weeks. Englewood Cliffs, N. J.: Prentice- Hall, Inc. 1962, p. 36.

10 See "Hemingway and the Thing Left Out," by Julian Smith in Linda Wagner's *Ernest Hemingway: Five Decades of Criticism*. n. p. Michigan State University Press, 1974, p. 188.

11 Ernest Hemingway to Bernard Berenson, 27 May 53. I am indebted to Dr. Cecil Anrep of I Tatti, for providing a copy of this letter.

12 Ernest Hemingway to Malcom Cowley, August, 1952. This unpublished letter is quoted in part in my essay, "Invention from Knowledge: The Hemingway-Cowley Correspondence," in *Ernest*

Hemingway: The Writer in Context, ed. James Nagel. Madison: University of Wisconsin Press, 1984, p.223.

13   *A Moveable Feast,* p.91.

14   *Letters,* p. 808

15   Ernest Hemingway to Edward J O'Brien, 12 Sept. 1924, Letters, p. 123.

16   For an extended discussion of Hemingway's concept of invention, see my essay in Nagel, pp.201-236.

17   Hemingway's affinity to James is becoming increasingly obvious as he becomes a candidate for James' portrait of the ideal writer in "The Art of Fiction." See Adeline Tintner, "Ernest and Henry: Hemingway's Lover's Quarrel with James," *Ernest Hemingway: The Writer in Context.* Ed. James Nagel. Madison: The University of Wisconsin Press, 1984. pp. 165-178.

18   Ernest Hemingway to Bernard Berenson, 13 Sept.1952, *Letters,* p.780.

19   See note # 13.

20   Hemingway had acquired a specialist's library on fishes. See James D. Brasch and Joseph Sigman. *Hemingway's Library: A Composite List.* New York: Garland Publishing, Inc., 1981.

21   14 Oct 1952, *Letters,* p.789.

22   Roll 19, # 845

23   *Ernest Hemingway: The Nick Adams Stories.* New York: Bantam Books, 1973, p.217.

24   Ernest Hemingway to Bernard Berenson, 24 Sept 1954, *Letters,* p. 836.

25   Ernest Hemingway to Charles Poore, 23 Jan 1952, *Letters,* p. 800.

26   Ernest Hemingway to Charles Poore, 23-28 Feb 1953. See *Hemingway at Auction,* ed. Matthew J Bruccoli and Frazer Clark. Detroit: Gale Research Co., 1973. p. 168.

27   Ernest Hemingway to Charles Poore, 23 Sept 1951.

28   Ernest Hemingway to Charles Atkins, 24 Oct. 1951.

29   *The Apprenticeship of Ernest Hemingway: The Early Years:.* New York: The Viking Press, 1954.

30   *Apprenticeship,* p. ix..

31   *In the Cage and Other Tales,* ed. Morton D. Zabel. New York: Doubleday Anchor Books, 1958, p.297.

32   *The Garden of Eden* was presented as Hemingway's novel if one is to judge by the printed text, but was actually edited by Scribners' Ed. Tom Jenks who reduced 1500 pages of manuscript to 247 pages by omitting at least one major character and a sub-plot and other text.

33   See Daniel J. Schneider, "Hemingway's Farewell to Arms: The Novel as Pure Poetry," in *Ernest Hemingway: Five Decades of Criticism*, Michigan State University Press, 1974, pp. 252-266.

34   Wallace Stevens to Henry Church, 2 July 42. *Letters of Wallace Stevens*, Selected and edited by Holly Stevens. New York: Alfred A. Knopf, 1966, pp. 411-12. Stevens' emphasis.

35   Ernest Hemingway, *88 Poems*, ed. with intro. by Nicholas Gerogiannis (New York, 1979), p. xi.

36   "Edition unknown" indicates that the original Cuban inventory did not record details of publication. For a complete description of all of our sources see Hemingway's Library (1981).

37   Mary Hemingway, *How It Was*. New York, 1976, p. 428.

Notes for Chapter 3

1   Carlos Baker, Charles Scribner's Sons, 1969, pp. 374,447,484,486,653.

2   Iuri Nikolaevich Paparov, *Kheminguei na Kube*. Ocherki, Moskva: Sovietski Pisatiel, 1979,

3   I am indebted to my former colleague, Prof. Emeritas Earl Hampel who generously devoted much time to translating Dr Herrera's rather patrician diction and style

4   This magazine, no longer published, was circulated with Toronto's *The Globe and Mail*, September 4, 1971. The article was entitled "As if Hemingway Might Stride in at Any Moment, Pour Himself a Gin and Tonic and...." I am indebted to Graham for providing me with her original manuscript and informal notes.

5   Mary Cruz to JDB, Feb 18, 1984.

6   Recently, Lyle Stuart of Secaucus, New Jersey, has published an altered and expurgated edition of Norberto Fuentes' *Hemingway in Cuba* which was allegedly written primarily while Fuentes was on assignment with Cuban troops in Angola. Fuentes quotes from Cunill's interview with Herrera, but does not credit Cunill for the interview and pretends that he is conducting the interview about ten years later than it originally took place. Fuentes has evidently supplemented the interview with additional information, but his record of Hemingway's life in Cuba is so replete with factual errors and propaganda for the Cuban revolution that his contributions to Hemingway's biography are negligible.

7   A. E. Hotchner, *Papa Hemingway* New York: Random House, 1966.

8   Paparov, pp.215-18.

9   Although the movement did not take its revolutionary form until
    Castro broke with the Ortodoxo Party on March 19, 1956, the "26th
    of July Movement" records the date in 1955 on which the ferryboat,
    Pinero, returned the [relatively] unknown Castro and his comrades
    to the mainland from the Isle of Pines after they had been granted
    amnesty. Fidel Castro and his supporters had been arrested following
    their attack on the Moncado Barracks.

10 Baker, Carlos, ed. *Ernest Hemingway: Selected Letters, 1917-1961*,
    Charles Scribner's Sons, 1981. p. 513.

11 Baker, *loc.cit.*

12 Edmundo Desnoes, *Inconsolable Memories* (New American Library,
    1967), pp. 70-71.

13 Herbert L. Matthews, *Fidel Castro* New York:Simon and Schuster,
    1969, pp. 180-81.

14 Paparov, p. 401.

15 Reported in *The New York Times*, August 22, 1957, p. 8.

16 Paparov, p. 403.

17 See Baker, pp. 464, 500. Baker records that the dog was brought from
    Idaho in 1948 and that it had been a loyal servant, but he omits any
    mention of the violent death.

18 *Letters*, p. 890.

19 Baker, p. 551. Paparov's version of this same incident translates, "I
    kissed it as an expression from my heart, not as an artist" (410-12).

20 Paparov, p. 407. There is considerable confusion about this article,
    and I include it here to invite further information on its origin, its
    authenticity, and its exact contents. Herrera insists that it appeared
    first in a Ketchum, Idaho, newspaper [possibly the *Wood River
    Journal*, published in Hailey, Idaho] and that it was subsequently
    suppressed by the American press (Cunill, Cruz). Paparov writes
    that it was a New York Times article and that Castro had received a
    copy of it from a sympathizer in Paraguay. So far diligent search has
    not produced the article, and the possibility that it is a fabrication
    must be entertained.

21 Euclides Vasquez-Candela, "Hemingway se preocupa por Cuba y
    por Fidel," *Gaceta de Cuba*, La Habana, 11:3 February 1963, 8-9. See
    also Paparov, pp. 407-08.

22 See his letter to Arthur Mizener, 12 May 1950, *Letters*, p. 694,
    and James D. Brasch and Joseph Sigman, *Hemingway's Library: A
    Composite Record* New York:Garland Press, 1981, which lists over
    fifty volumes devoted to the American Civil War.

23 Baker, p. 552.

24   For a sympathetic account of this meeting, see Sergi Mikoyan, "Anastas
      Mikoyan Meets Ernest Hemingway," *Kroonk* (Committee for Cultural
      Relations with Armenians Abroad), No.3 (1984), pp. 22-26.
25   Paparov, p. 412.
26   Baker, p. 552.

Notes for Chapter 4

1   From *Blue Juniata: Collected Poems* (New York: Viking, 1968), p. 96.
      This poem was reprinted with the permission of Malcolm Cowley.
2   Ernest Hemingway to Malcolm Cowley, 16 September 1951 I read
      these letters through the generosity and hospitality of Marsha and
      Maurice Neville. In 1984 the letters were sold at auction and the
      present owner (not identified) refuses access and will not reveal their
      location.
3   See James D. Brasch and Joseph Sigman, "Reading Habits,"
      Hemingway's Library: A Composite Record (New York: Garland,
      1981), p. xviii. Hemingway's library contained considerable
      material by Cowley: Exile's Return: A Literary Odyssey of the 1920's
      (1951); The Literary Situation (1954); After the Genteel Tradition:
      American Writers since 1910 (1937) (2 copies); The Stories of F.
      Scott Fitzgerald: A Selection of 28 Stories, Introduction by Malcolm
      Cowley (1951); Tender Is the Night, with the author's final revsions,
      preface by Malcolm Cowley (1951); Andre Gide, Imaginary
      Interviews, translated from the French by Malcolm Cowley (1944);
      Interviews, edited with an introduction by Malcolm Cowley (1958);
      Robert Terrall, ed., Great Scenes from Great Novels, Introduction by
      Malcolm Cowley (1956); The Portable Faulkner (1946), The Portable
      Hawthorne (1948), and The Portable Hemingway (1944), all selected
      and edited by Malcolm Cowley.
4   "Nightmare and Ritual in Hemingway," Introduction to *The Portable
      Hemingway*, ed. Malcolm Cowley (New York: Viking, 1945).
      Malcolm Cowley's introduction is reprinted in Robert P.Weeks,
      ed., *Hemingway: A Collection of Critical Essays* (Englewood Cliffs:
      Prentice-Hall, 1962). See also Malcolm Cowley to Ernest Hemingway,
      24 September 1949.
5   Malcolm Cowley, "A Portrait of Mr. Papa," *Life*, 10 January 1949, pp.
      86-101. This essay is reprinted in John K. M. McCaffery, ed., *Ernest
      Hemingway: The Man and His Work* Cleveland: World, 1950.
6   Only two of Hemingway's letters to Cowley were included in
      Carlos Baker's *Ernest Hemingway: Selected Letters, 1917-1961* (New

York:, Scribner's, 1981). Maurice Neville's longstanding interest in Hemingway's works and generosity enabled me to study these letters. Peter Buckley, a longtime friend of Hemingway's, generously brought the letters to my attention. I am also indebted to Alfred Rice of the Hemingway Foundation for permission to quote excerpts from Hemingway's letters to Cowley. Mr. Cowley has encouraged me and graciously assisted in this assessment of the correspondence. He also deposited copies of thirteen letters which he sent to Hemingway in the Hemingway Collection of the John F. Kennedy Library, Boston, Mass. Jo August Hills, a former curator of the Hemingway Collection, facilitated my examination of these copies.

7   For a useful discussion of "invention" (Latin: *inventio*) as defined and applied by Aristotle and Cicero with an indication of more recent implications, see Edward P. J. Corbett, *Classical Rhetoric for the Modern Student* . New York: Oxford University Press, 1971, pp. 33-39, *et passim. Inventio* was concerned with a system or method for finding arguments (subject matter to illustrate or support a speaker's point of view).

8   Ernest Hemingway to Malcolm Cowley, 19 August 1948.

9   Ernest Hemingway to Malcolm Cowley, 16 September 1951.

10   Hemingway also found it necessary to explain his position to John Atkins (*The Art of Ernest Hemingway* [London: P. Nevill, 1952]): "I have refused to cooperate with anyone writing any sort of biography as there are too many people involved in my life to write about it truly. Also it makes me sick to read about it, true or false. My work is all 1 give a damn about and so many people have tried to pull my life (good, bad or worse) into all criticism of it that now a book of mine is judged by some people on whether 1 hit some man in a place like the Stork Club (after being goaded into it), than on the merits or demerits of the book."

"Cowley came down here to write something about me for Life .... 1 found that after the first night 1 talked with him that it made me feel truly nauseated to talk about myself, and 1 compromised by giving him a list of people 1 had served under or with or who had known me at different times in my life. It was from this material and from others who claimed to know me that he wrote the article which appeared in Life and McCaffery [*Ernest Hemingway: The Man and His Work*]. It would take many letters to tell you how accurate or inaccurate it is and then 1 might be wrong. Any man is liable to be prejudiced about his life, since he knows things about it that as kind and good a critic as Cowley would never understand." Ernest Hemingway to John Atkins, 24 October 1951.

11   Ernest Hemingway to Malcolm Cowley, 10 February 1949.

12   Ernest Hemingway to Malcolm Cowley, 9 March 1949. *Vogue* played a particularly dirty trick on him, and his work was not only disturbed, but other vibrations resulted as well: For instance, an editor of *Vogue* called up and got through on the phone by saying she was the wife of one of my best friends. This was the entering wedge. Was untrue, of course; then she asked to bring a model out to make some fashion pictures using the *Finca* for background shots. I said sure to be accommodating and because I hadn't seen a really pretty girl since Mary went north to settle her parents in Gulfport. So they took some pictures of the model and me just after they had finished their work. They said these were just personal for ourselves and not to be published. In two months, they were in *Vogue*. The one they published was in *Vogue* with me lying on a couch with only shorts on with a very beautiful and nice girl who is in *Vogue* every month and on the covers half the time and looking down at me. This thing does you a lot of good around the house. (Ernest Hemingway to Malcolm Cowley, 13 May 1951).

13   Hemingway wrote to Fenton: "Are you sure that you are quite all right in the head? The sudden rages and general truculence are disquieting in a scholar. I do not believe your university would approve of them nor of the tone of some of your letters" (Ernest Hemingway to Charles Fenton, 13 July 1952. Fenton was a particularly annoying problem for Hemingway. Hemingway wrote him again: "Many months ago I warned you to cease and desist on your project for writing a book on my literary and journalistic apprenticeship, which has degenerated or enlarged into a full scale invasion of privacy" (Ernest Hemingway to Charles Fenton, 10 February 1953.. See also Ernest Hemingway to Charles Fenton, 29 July 1952, 9 October 1952 (*Ernest Hemingway, Selected Letters*, pp. 774, 786); and Ernest Hemingway to Dorothy Connable, 17 February 1953: "Fenton is one of those who think that literary history, or the secret of creative writing, lies in old laundry lists" (*Ernest Hemingway, Selected Letters*, p. 805). In April 1953, Hemingway instructed his lawyer, Alfred Rice, to intervene (Ernest Hemingway to Alfred Rice, 26 and 27 April 1953 [Letters, p. 818]). Fenton's book, *The Apprenticeship of Ernest Hemingway: The Early Years,* was published in 1954 by Farrar, Straus & Young, New York.

14   Max Eastman and Edmund Wilson were constantly attacked by Hemingway because, in his opinion, they refused to admit to

mistakes and, therefore, were "the death of honest criticism." Ernest Hemingway to Malcolm Cowley, 3 September 1945.

15   Ernest Hemingway to Malcolm Cowley, 30 October 1947.

16   See Carlos Baker, *Ernest Hemingway: A Life Story*. New York: Scribner's, 1969, p. 464.

17   Malcolm Cowley to James D. Brasch, 23 December 1980.(in the possession of James D. Brasch..

18   Ernest Hemingway to Malcolm Cowley, 19 August 1948.

19   See *Baker, A Life Story*, pp. 408-10, *et passim.*

20   Malcolm Cowley to Ernest Hemingway, 18 April 1951, 9 May 1951, and 19 May 1951. Carbon copies of these letters are in the Hemingway Collection, John F. Kennedy Library.

21   Ernest Hemingway to Malcolm Cowley, 9 March 1949; Cowley's misinterpretation of the Oak Park 'years evidently upset Hemingway so much that Mary felt called upon to step in. Her letter to Cowley is included in the Neville collection. She pointed out a number of his errors and insisted that Cowley had heard reports which confused Hemingway with his brother Leicester (Mary Welsh Hemingway to Malcolm Cowley, 9 February 1949..

22   Ernest Hemingway to Malcolm Cowley, 10 June 1949.

23   Malcolm Cowley to Ernest Hemingway, 28 January 1952. A copy is in the Hemingway Collection, John F. Kennedy Library. Hemingway summarized his exasperation in two letters written directly to Bledsoe, 9 December 1951 *Letters*, pp. 743-46); and 17 and 31 January 1952 *Letters*, pp. 747-48).

24   Ernest Hemingway to Arthur Mizener, 4 January 1951, in *Letters*, p. 717.

25   Arthur Mizener, "F. Scott Fitzgerald's Tormented Paradise: The rediscovered novelist of the '20's was beset by drink, debt, a mad wife." *Life*, 15 January 1951, pp. 82-88.

26   Ernest Hemingway to Malcolm Cowley, 1 June 1951.

27   Ernest Hemingway to Malcolm Cowley, 19 April 1951.

28   Mizener had written in *Life*: "To the telling of this story [*The Great Gatsby*] Fitzgerald brought what Malcolm Cowley has called his 'double vision,' that special view in which he saw his own life: 'It was as if all his novels described a big dance to which he had taken … the prettiest girl … and as if at the same time he stood outside the ballroom, a little Midwestern boy with his nose to the glass, wondering how much the tickets cost and who paid for the music.'" "F. Scott Fitzgerald's Tormented Paradise," p. 101.

29   Ernest Hemingway to Malcolm Cowley, 8 November 1951.

30   Ernest Hemingway to Malcolm Cowley, 8 November 1951.
31   F. Scott Fitzgerald, Tender Is the Night, republished "With the Author's Final Revisions," ed. Malcolm Cowley (New York: Scribner's, 1951).
32   Ernest Hemingway to Malcolm Cowley, 20 November 1951.
33   Ernest Hemingway, A Moveable Feast (New York: Scribner's, 1964).
34   Ernest Hemingway, A Moveable Feast Manuscript. Kennedy Library Roll 19, Target 171, Hemingway Collection, John F. Kennedy Library.
35   Ernest Hemingway to Malcolm Cowley, 16 September 1951.
36   Hemingway's view of Cowley as an editor must be taken in the context of a projected three-volume edition of A Farewell to Arms, The Sun Also Rises, and For Whom the Bell Tolls concocted by Perkins, Cowley, and Hemingway, to be edited by Cowley. See Ernest Hemingway to Charles Scribner, 28 June 1947, in Letters, pp.621-23.
37   Hemingway wrote to Arthur Mizener: "Fitzgerald was romantic, ambitious, and Christ, Jesus, God knows how talented .... He was uneducated and refused to educate himself in any way. He would make great studies about football, say, and war but it was all bullshit .... Above all he was completely undisciplined." Ernest Hemingway to Arthur Mizener, 22 April 1950, in Ernest Hemingway, Selected Letters, p. 690.
38   Ernest Hemingway to Malcolm Cowley, 16 September 1951.
39   Ernest Hemingway to Malcolm Cowley, 16 September 1951.
40   Ernest Hemingway to Malcolm Cowley, 20 November 1951.
41   Ernest Hemingway to Malcolm Cowley, 16 November 1948.
42   Ernest Hemingway to Malcolm Cowley, 24 July 1951.
43   Hemingway to Malcolm Cowley, 16 September 1951.
44   Life, 1 September 1952, pp. 35-54.
45   Jay Leyda, The Melville Log, 2 vols. New York: Harcourt, Brace, 1951.
46   Malcolm Cowley to Ernest Hemingway, 3 November 1951. A carbon copy is in the Hemingway Collection, John F. Kennedy Library.
47   Malcolm Cowley to Ernest Hemingway, 3 November 1951. A carbon copy is in the Hemingway Collection, John F. Kennedy Library.
48   Malcolm Cowley to Ernest Hemingway, 3 November 1951. A carbon copy is in the Hemingway Collection, John F. Kennedy Library.
49   Ernest Hemingway to Malcolm Cowley, 8 November 1951.
50   Ernest Hemingway to Malcolm Cowley, 20 November 1951.
51   About the same time, Hemingway was trying to explain to John Atkins how he had invented the character of Col. Cantwell in Across the River and into the Trees (1950): Col. Buck Lanham was my best

friend and we went through many strange things together. He was also a poet, a lover of pictures, and literature and a man of violent opinions. I used some of his characteristics and some of four other colonels or generals I knew (two of them) and of them since the First War in inventing that Colonel Cantwell everyone hated so much .... If anything I knew too much, rather than too little about war from platoons through company battalion, regimental and divisional level. (Ernest Hemingway to John Atkins, 28 December 1952).

52   This essay is readily available in *The Portable Henry James,* ed. Morton Zabel (New York: Viking, 1956), pp. 391-418.

53   Ernest Hemingway to Malcolm Cowley, 29 May 1952.

54   See note 3 and Michael S. Reynolds, *Hemingway's Reading, 1910-1940:* An Inventory (Princeton: Princeton University Press, 1981).

55   Ernest Hemingway to Malcolm Cowley, 10 February 1949.

56   See Norman Mailer, *The Naked and the Dead.*New York: New American Library, 1951, p. 99.

57   Ernest Hemingway to Malcolm Cowley, 10 February 1949.

58   Malcolm Cowley to Ernest Hemingway, 3 August 1952.

59   Ernest Hemingway to Malcolm Cowley, August 1952.

60   Malcolm Cowley to Ernest Hemingway, 3 August 1952.

61   Ernest Hemingway to Malcolm Cowley, August 1952.

62   Ernest Hemingway to Malcolm Cowley, August 1952.

63   Ernest Hemingway to Malcolm Cowley, August 1952.

64   Malcolm Cowley to Ernest Hemingway, 3 August 1952.

65   Ernest Hemingway to Malcolm Cowley, August 1952.

66   Ernest Hemingway to Malcolm Cowley, August 1952.

67   Hemingway's library contained over 225 books on fishing, including three on marlin classification (see note 3).

68   Ernest Hemingway to Malcolm Cowley, August 1952.

69   See Emily Stipes Watts, *Ernest Hemingway and the Arts* (Urbana: University of Illinois Press, 1971); and Meyle Chin Hagemann, "Hemingway's Secret: Visual to Verbal Art," *Journal of Modern Literature* 7, 1979,pp. 87-112.

70   Malcolm Cowley, "Hemingway's Novel Has the Rich Simplicity of a Classic," Sunday, 7 September 1952, pp. 1, 17. Cowley explained the cessation this way: "Memory tells me, beyond a shadowy doubt, that the correspondence ended quite explicably. There had been a fight about the Oak Park section of my LIFE article, which was based on material dug up for me by old Otto McFeeley, who had edited The Oak Leaf when Ernest delivered it as a boy. What I said was absolutely accurate, except that I had softened the statements made

by McFeeley so that they wouldn't hurt Ernest. He was hurt all the same, and angry, but we smoothed things over. The final breaking-off came as an indirect result of Philip Young's biography, about which Ernest was greatly exercised .... After that we exchanged nothing but Christmas cards, and not every year" (Malcolm Cowley to James D. Brasch, 11 May 1982, in the possession of James D. Brasch).

71 Cowley, "Hemingway's Novel," p. 1.

72 Cowley, "Hemingway's Novel," p. 17.

73 Cowley, "Hemingway's Novel," p. 17.

74 Cowley, "Hemingway's Novel," p. 17.

75 Ernest Hemingway to Malcolm Cowley, 4 May 1952; letter sent 15 May 1952.

76 Ernest Hemingway to Charles Poore, 23 January 1953, in Ernest Hemingway, Selected Letters, p. 800.

77 Malcolm Cowley to Conrad Aiken, 7 July 1961, in the Huntington Library, Pasadena, Calif. Cowley's admiration for Hemingway's knowledge was a recurring theme of his two chapters, "Hemingway in Paris" and "Hemingway the Old Lion," in *A Second Flowering: Works and Days of the Lost Generation.*New York: Viking, 1973).

Notes for Chapter 5

1 Fuentes, 1984.

2 Brasch, 1986. (See chapter 3)

3 Ernest Hemingway to Bernard Berenson, 11 Aug, 1953; at sea.

4 Ernest Hemingway to Bernard Berenson, 17 Feb., 1963.

5 See, for example, *Conoisseur*, Oct., 1986, "The Berenson scandal," pp. 126-38 and Colin Simpson, *Artful Partners: Bernard Berenson and Joseph Duveen*, New York: Macmilan, 1986.

6 Baker, 1969, p. 527.

7 Mary Welsh Hemingway, 1976, p. 231.

8 Ernest Hemingway to Bernard Berenson, 20 March, 1953.

9 Ernest Hemingway to Bernard Berenson, 2 March 1956,

10 Ernest Hemingway to Bernard Berenson, 13 Sept., 1952.

11 Meyers, 1986, p. 429.

12 I am indebted to the late Cecil Anrep for permission to read Hemingway's letters to Berenson and for providing me with copies of the letters. These letters are now under administrations of Harvard University. I would also like to thank Dottoressa Fiorella Geoffredi-Superbi who graciously assisted my reexamination of the letters including the many articles attached to the original letters. My

thanks also to the staff of *Villa 'I Tatti"* (now the Harvard University Center for Renaissance Studies) for giving me access during July 1986 to the correspondence between Martha Gellhorn and Bernard Berenson and Berenson's books by Hemingway.

13 Mary Hemingway to Bernard Berenson, 21 August, 1957.

14 Secrest, p. 13.

15 Bernard Berenson to Ernest Hemingway, 22 June, 1953.

16 Bernard Berenson to Ernest Hemingway, 26 March 1954; Berenson's emphasis.

17 Ernest Hemingway to Bernard Berenson, 22 January 1954.

18 Bernard Berenson to Ernest Hemingway, 22 December 1954.

19 Baker 1981, p. 667.

20 Ernest Hemingway to Bernard Berenson, 6 March 1953.

21 Ernest Hemingway to Bernard Berenson, 18 Sept, 1955.

22 Ernest Hemingway to Bernard Berenson, 20 March 1953.

23 Ernest Hemingway to Bernard Berenson, 11 August 1953.

24 Ernest Hemingway to Bernard Berenson, 4 Oct. 1955.

25 Ernest Hemingway to Bernard Berenson, 4 May 1953.

26 Bernard Berenson to Ernest Hemingway, 22 Dec. 1954.

27 Ernest Hemingway to Bernard Berenson, 10 June 1953.

28 Ernest Hemingway to Bernard Berenson, 17 Feb. 1953.

29 Bernard Berenson to Ernest Hemingway, 22 June 1953.

30 Bernard Berenson to Ernest Hemingway, 29 March 1953.

31 Bernard Berenson to Ernest Hemingway, 29 March 1953.

32 Bernard Berenson to Ernest Hemingway, 15 March 1953.

33 Ernest Hemingway to Bernard Berenson, 10 June 1953.

34 Ernest Hemingway to Bernard Berenson, 21 March 1953.

35 Bernard Berenson to Ernest Hemingway, 15 March 1953.

36 Ernest Hemingway to Bernard Berenson, 20 March 1953.

37 Ernest Hemingway to Bernard Berenson, 2 Feb. 1954.

38 Ernest Hemingway to Bernard Berenson, 20 March 1953.

39 Ernest Hemingway to Bernard Berenson, 21 March 1953.

40 Ernest Hemingway to Bernard Berenson, 4 Oct., 1955.

41 Ernest Hemingway to Bernard Berenson, 24 Sept., 1954.

42 Secrest, 1979, p. 219.

43 Ernest Hemingway to Bernard Berenson, 20 March, 1953; 27 May 1953.

44 Ernest Hemingway to Bernard Berenson, 20 March 1953.

45 Ernest Hemingway to Bernard Berenson, 24 September 1954.

46 *Ibid.*

47 Ernest Hemingway to Bernard Berenson, 14 Oct. 1952.

48 Ernest Hemingway to Bernard Berenson, 27 May 1953.
49 Bernard Berenson to Ernest Hemingway, 17 Sept. 1954.
50 Bernard Berenson to Ernest Hemingway, 6 Sept. 1952.
51 Ernest Hemingway to Bernard Berenson, 13 Sept., 1952.
52 *Ibid.*
53 Cable to Rupert Belleville, Whites, London, 9 Sept., 1952.
54 See, for example, *The New York Times*, Nov. 10, 1952, p.23.
55 Mary Welsh Hemingway, 1976, p. 230.
56 Secrest 1979, p.12.
57 Bernard Berenson to Ernest Hemingway, 15 March 1953.
58 See Baker 1969, p. 508.
59 Bernard Berenson to Ernest Hemingway, 15 March 1953.
60 Bernard Berenson to Ernest Hemingway, 21 May 1953.
61 Martha Gelhorn to Bernard Berenson, 26 April 1954.
62 Ernest Hemingway to Bernard Berenson, 10 June 1953.
63 Ernest Hemingway to Bernard Berenson, 27 May 1953.
64 Ernest Hemingway to Bernard Berenson, 27 May 1953.
65 *Ibid.*
66 Ernest Hemingway to Bernard Berenson, 19 Aug 1956.
67 Ernest Hemingway to Bernard Berenson, 27 May 1953.
68 Ernest Hemingway to Bernard Berenson, 27 May 1953.
69 Bernard Berenson to Ernest Hemingway, 10 Oct. 1952.
70 Ernest Hemingway to Bernard Berenson, 10 April 1956.
71 Ernest Hemingway to Bernard Berenson, 30 April 1957.
72 Ernest Hemingway to Bernard Berenson, 9 April 1954.
73 Ernest Hemingway to Bernard Berenson, 22 March 1953.
74 Secrest 1979, p. 376.
75 Bernard Berenson to Ernest Hemingway, 2 Nov. 1955.

Reference Bibliography:

Baker, Carlos. *Ernest Hemingway: A Life Story*. New York: Scribner, 1969.

_____*Ernest Hemingway: Selected Letters*. 1917-1961. New York: Scribner, 1981.

Berenson, Bernard. *Sunset and Twilight*. ed. Nicky Mariano. New York: Harcourt, 1963.

Brasch, James D. "The Watershed in Hemingway Criticism," *The Canadian Review of American Studies*, Volume IX, Number 1, Spring, 1978.

_____(review of) *Hemingway and Faulkner; Inventors/Masters* by Linda Welshimer Wagner. Metuchen, N.J.: The Scarecrow Press, 1975.

_____"Hemingway's Words: Enduring James's Thoughts: a Review Essay," *Modernist Studies, Literature and Culture 1920-1940*.

_____(with Joseph Sigman)Introduction to *Hemingway's Library; A Composite Record*. New York: Garland, 1981

_____(with Joseph Sigman)"Hemingway's Library: Some Volumes of Poetry" , *College Literature*, Vol. VII. 3. 1980.

_____"Hemingway's 'Realer Than Real, Truer Than True'", *Chiba Review*, #9: Tokyo, 1987.

_____"Christ, I wish I could Paint: The Correspondence between Ernest Hemingway and Bernard Berenson," *Hemingway in Italy and Other Essays,* Ed. Robert W. Lewis. New York: Praeger, 1990.

_____"Hemingway's Doctor: Jose Luis Herrera   Sotolongo Remembers Ernest Hemingway", *Journal of Modern Literature*, Vol. 13, No. 2, July, 1986.

_____"Invention from Knowledge: The Hemingway/Cowley Correspondence." *Ernest Hemingway: The Writer in Context*. Madison: The University of Wisconsin Press, Ed. James Nagel, 1984.

_____ (with Joseph Sigman)"Art at Finca Vigia: A Cuban Caricature of Hemingway" *The Hemingway Review*, Vol 11. Fall. 1982..

_____ (with Joseph Sigman)*Hemingway's Library: A   Composite Record*,   New York: Garland Publishing Co. 1981.

_____ (with Joseph Sigman) "The Library at Finca Vigia: A Preliminary Report", 1977. *Fitgerald/Hemingway Annual, 1978*, ed. Matthew J Brocoli and Richard Layman. Detroit, Michigan: Gale Research Co., 1979.

Fuentes, Norberto. *Hemingway in Cuba*. Secaucus, NJ: Lyle Stuart, 1984.

Hemingway, Mary Welsh. *How It Was*. New York: Knopf, 1976.

Meyers, Jeffrey. *Hemingway: A Biography*. New York: Harper & Row, 1986.

Paparov, Iuri.Nikolaevich,*Hemingway na Kube* (Ocherki, Moskva: Sovietski Pisatiel, 1979.

Secrest, Meryle. *Being Bernard Berenson*. New York: Holt, 1979.

Watts, Emily Stipes. *Ernest Hemingway and the Arts*. Urbana, Ill. University of Illinois Press, 1971.

Author biography:

James D Brasch is a founding member of the Hemingway Society and in 1984 was the General Chairman of the First International Hemingway Conference in Madrid, Spain. He taught American Literature at McMaster University, Hamilton, Ontario, Canada for 30 years. In 1976 Mary Hemingway selected him and a colleague to produce a catalogue of Hemingway's library(1981) mostly in *Finca Vigia* in Cuba

He is now retired and lives in Burlington, Ontario with his wife and chief critic, Delores.